ANSWERS TO THE
QUESTIONS CHRISTIAN WOMEN ARE ASKING

Bill & Nancie Carmichael

HARVEST HOUSE PUBLISHERS
Eugene, Oregon 97402

ᴜxcept where otherwise indicated, all Scripture quotations in this
book are taken from the King James Version of the Bible.

**ANSWERS TO THE QUESTIONS
CHRISTIAN WOMEN ARE ASKING**

Copyright © 1984 by Harvest House Publishers
Eugene, Oregon 97402

Library of Congress Catalog Card Number 84-81213
ISBN 0-89081-442-2

Printed in the United States of America.

We lovingly dedicate this book to you, Christian woman.

The more we know you, the more we admire...

- Your desire to know your God...
- Your willingness to study His written Word...
- Your tenacious stand to make your family your first priority...
- Your rejection of any evil that would invade your home...
- Your courageous efforts at personal growth...
- Your ability to see God in the ordinary things of your life.

For these beautiful qualities, we say "Thank you." Truly you are light and salt in our world!

—Bill and Nancie Carmichael

Our Special Thanks To...

...the fine people at Harvest House Publishers for being so helpful...Paul Johnson, M.D., for his medical expertise ...Diane Nason for help with adoption facts...the *Virtue/Solo* staff for moral support and encouragement...friends and relatives who helped babysit...Mom and Dad Carmichael and Mom Pearson for being interested...Missy Kitchell, Janice Lovegren, and Donna Anderson for typing ...and last but not least, special thanks to our five wonderful children: Jon, Eric, Chris, Andy, and Amy for being patient with Mom and Dad during "the summer of the book"!

PREFACE

Over the years of publishing *Virtue* magazine and speaking to a variety of groups and churches, we have listened to Christian women share their hearts, asking us for answers to some very serious questions.

Often these women have expressed the discomfort of going to their pastor or friend for fear that their "deep secret" will be misunderstood or be passed on to someone else. Some fear outright rejection. Many come from small towns where there are no professional Christian counselors. Still others have received bad advice by well-meaning but inadequately informed people.

The purpose of this book is to help point these women in the right direction. Our answers are neither exhaustive nor final. Obviously one cannot "solve" a problem in a few pages, or even a whole book. Problems are best solved when shared with a caring, loving, knowledgeable Christian who is willing to listen and use the gentle leading of the Holy Spirit and the authoritative Word of God to counsel.

The answers in this book are designed to point you in the right direction. We have tried with each question to give some facts about the subject, some Scriptural encouragement, some practical advice we have gleaned from our experience and the experiences of others, and some resources showing where you can find additional help.

Space does not allow including every question that could be asked, but it is a comfort to know that God provides a way through every crisis, every problem, every mistake, every failure, every heartache. Keep searching and reaching out to God. After all, He is our ultimate Source. He *does* have the answer!

—*BILL & NANCIE CARMICHAEL*

CONTENTS

IV. HEALTH

V. PARENT/CHILD RELATIONSHIPS

Part I_____

Marriage & Sexual
Relationships

QUESTION 1

> ### *How can I encourage my husband to communicate with me?*

To *communicate* means to "convey information, make known, converse, share with another person what is primarily one's own." What you want is for your husband to share what is "his own"—his thoughts, feelings, and emotions—what he is inside. Our society doesn't make it easy for men to open up. Some men have the idea that a "real man" is the strong, solitary cowboy, the macho hero. Some men are afraid of intimacy because they're afraid to be vulnerable, to show weakness, to become dependent.

It seems easier for women to open up. If two women friends have lunch together and one asks the other, "How *are* you?" her friend begins responding with how she's been feeling. If two men friends have lunch together and one asks the other, "How are *you?*" his friend probably replies by giving him facts about his work, recreation, and so on.

It's very appealing to a woman to have a man open up to her. It's a delicate process in marriage, one that doesn't happen overnight. Bill and I have spent 18 years developing "soul" communication. At this point in our marriage we enjoy an intimacy that amazes us. We are grateful to God! If two imperfect human beings with such different personalities as ours can learn to communicate, any couple can!

"You can trace the degree to which two people are becoming intimate," says Dr. Loy McGinnis, a marriage counselor, "by watching how their talk moves from factual information to intimate revelation. Generally, new acquaintances

13

restrict their conversation to facts; but as they know each other better, they begin to trust each other with opinion; finally, if they have become genuine friends, emotions will emerge."[1]

Perhaps one of the most beautiful qualities to develop in marriage is this sense of friendship. Bill is my best friend. We've been through good times and bad times, and we still love and respect one another. Here are some principles we have learned in our quest for communication.

1. *Learning how to meet our deepest needs.* There have been times when I could not "reach" Bill, but I saw how he found a quiet place with his Bible, or knew he was spending extra time in prayer and soul-searching. There have been times when I had to get alone with God for some specific answers and direction. These are times—other than regular devotional times—when we are reminded that it is only in our personal relationships with God that we find security and total acceptance.

We cannot always expect this from each other in the deepest sense. We are finite beings. God is the only One who can offer us ultimate fulfillment. In Him we are complete. We must always keep going back to the source—our Creator, who made us and knows us intimately. In other words, it is risky business to expect your husband to fulfill all your emotional needs.

2. *Learning to understand and love each other for who we are.* When we are secure in ourselves and in our personal relationships with God, then we are able to love one another with an attitude of acceptance and tolerance for each other's faults (Ephesians 4:32). When Bill knows without a doubt that I really love him with an "open arms" kind of love, then he feels free to open up to me. If my communication consists of "You need to do this" or "You shouldn't make comments like that," he clams up. He feels on trial, as if he must maintain a certain level of performance to be acceptable to me. That's a discouraging requirement!

Paul Tournier, an eminent Swiss psychiatrist, said, "Often

men are just as easily hurt as women, even though they hide it. They are afraid of being hurt by advice just as much as by criticism. They resent it every bit as much. A woman for whom everything seems clear-cut who confidently tells her husband how he must act in order to do the right thing, no matter what the problem might be. . .such a woman gives her husband the impression that she thinks him incompetent."[2] None of us is perfect, but it has been said that unless one feels accepted, it's hard for one to change.

3. *Learning to choose the right time and place.* Just as a rosebud needs gentle sun and rain to blossom, a relationship needs nurturing. It personally helps me to get my husband away from the house in order to get him to talk and then to listen. Our five children are very involved in many activities. If I'm not careful, my husband can view me as a "ship with a lot of barnacles"! We need to get away from the everyday and ordinary to see each other as sweethearts and confidantes rather than Mom and Dad and Provider and Cook. Bill and I like to take daily walks. It gives us a better perspective on the day, and we are able to enjoy each other as people who care very much about each other. It doesn't take long, about a half-hour, and it's great exercise.

Get away for a weekend, overnight, or just out to dinner. This is so basic that it seems like a cliche! And yet it is necessary. How many times have we heard that we must take time to read the Bible and pray? We know we must schedule time alone with God. Jesus said, "Where your treasure is, there will your heart be also" (Matthew 6:21). In other words, what you value, you will make a priority. If you value your marriage, you will prove it by the time you give your husband.

4. *Encouraging him to talk.* You can't expect meaningful dialogues with your husband if he's tired and hungry, and the kids have just burst in the door. You can set the stage, however. Physical needs have to be met—a meal prepared, a table set, an orderly home, and soft music in the background. All these things are soothing to the senses and help

one relax. It's hard to open up when one is uptight and burdened with pressures of life. Men need a sense of tranquility at home. Be sensitive to little things that are pleasant, that say "You're special." Provide a cup of hot tea or a gentle backrub. Don't be afraid to give him some time alone. Sometimes silence *is* golden! Later is the time to take his hand and say, "Honey, can you sit down and talk with me?" Ask his opinion about some matters you've been wanting to discuss, or share some concerns in a nonaccusing, nonthreatening way. Ask, "How do you feel about—" and then listen to him with your heart as well as your ears.

5. *Encouraging him to listen.* Some of us have more problems than others in getting people to listen to us. Maybe it's the way we're talking. Some of us talk too much without really saying what's on our heart! Here's some good advice from the Bible: "Let your speech be always with grace, seasoned with salt, that you may know how you ought to answer every man" (Colossians 4:6). "Let no corrupt communication proceed out of your mouth, but that which is good to the use of edifying, that it may minister grace to the hearers" (Ephesians 4:29).

There is a subtle attitude in a woman that makes a difference in a man's response to her. To encourage intimacy with your husband, Dr. Kiev says, "You have to be both independent and giving. People think those are contradictory, but they're not—*if* you're independent and giving in the right ways. Instead, most women react to a closed man by being dependent and demanding. . . . What does it mean to be independent and giving in the day-to-day business of a relationship? It means to have the emotional independence to *let* him be distant when he's in a bad mood (even if she's in a bad mood too), to let him complain when he's had a hard day (even if she's had a hard day too), and to let him have moments of privacy (because she needs them too). It means fighting the tendency to revert to dependent or demanding behavior when the level of his emotional giving falls below the level of her emotional need. . . . By being dependent and demanding," says Kiev, "a woman *invites* a man to withdraw emotionally. The moment she becomes independent, elusive and mysterious, a man will climb mountains to go after her."[3]

Honesty about our feelings in marriage is necessary, but the ethic of honesty must give way to a higher ethic of love. Ephesians 4:15 says that we should "grow up . . ." and learn to "speak the truth in love." There is a delicate balance here. We must have the courage to express our deepest feelings, and also to understand and read our husband's feelings—and then learn when to "back off."

It sometimes helps me to write down my feelings and give them to my husband. There have been times when I knew we *had* to get alone to find each other again, and I've had to "take the bull by the horns" and make babysitting arrangements or whatever it took to give us room to be together. However, there are times we need to ask ourselves, "Why am I feeling this way?" And maybe check the calendar! Some women suffer incredible tension during their menstrual cycle and dump a lot of unnecessary garbage on their husbands in the name of honesty.

But don't use this as an excuse to say, "Well, this is just the way I am, and that's the way he is. We aren't alike, and we just don't understand each other, so we'll each do our own thing." The loneliest people in the world—regardless of how many people they are surrounded by—are those who can't open up and really share who they are. The "real you" is buried beneath layers of pretense—an all-business attitude, a joking attitude, or a who-cares attitude. Maybe we're afraid to be vulnerable because we've been hurt and are afraid of getting hurt again. First John 4:18 says, "Perfect love casts out fear." Fear keeps us from growing old and reaching the full potential that God has for all of us.

One caution: If you've built up a lot of things inside, be careful about how you spill them out. For instance, it won't build a marriage to say, "I never *have* liked your family!" Communicate where you are and what you are without blaming or attacking. The idea is to build bridges toward each other. These bridges are made secure with honesty, caring, understanding, and effort.

RESOURCES

Talk to Me! Charlie W. Shedd. Jove Publishing, 1976.
The Marriage Builder. Lawrence Crabb, Jr. Zondervan.
Close Companions: The Marriage Enrichment Book. David Mace. Continuum Publishing Co., 1982.
Why Can't Men Open Up? Steven Naifeh and Gregory W. Smith. Clarkson Potter, Inc., 1984.
To Understand Each Other. Paul Tournier. John Knox Press.

NOTES

1. *Why Can't Men Open Up?* Steven Naifeh and Gregory W. Smith. Clarkson Potter, Inc., 1984.
2. *To Understand Each Other.* Paul Tournier. John Knox Press, 1967 (published in Switzerland in 1962), p. 24.
3. *Why Can't Men Open Up?* op. cit.

QUESTION 2

> **We have constant conflict in our marriage. I would like this to change.**

A certain amount of conflict in marriage is healthy. After all, marriage is made up of two unique, separate individuals! Ruth Bell Graham says in *My Side of the Story,* "In marriages where two people always agree, one is unnecessary!"[1]

But if the conflict is constant, always a tug-of-war, something is wrong. God created couples to experience "one-flesh" marriages. A good marriage has unity. Unity doesn't mean domination of one partner by the other. It doesn't mean dishonesty or hidden feelings. And it doesn't mean constant arguing! It means two people with the same purpose, going the same direction.

Whenever you get two individuals together for any length of time, you will eventually have differences of opinion. All of us, because of our unique backgrounds, genes, nationalities, temperaments, family influences, and spiritual depth, have different perspectives on life. To further complicate matters, we handle our disagreements differently. Some of us tend to be more open about our disagreements and displeasures. Others tend to suppress those feelings.

It has been a real education in our own marriage to learn how to handle conflict. Both of us had some work to do—myself in learning to express honest disagreement openly, and Bill in learning to temper his immediate reactions. I found in the earlier years of our marriage that frequently I would agree outwardly with Bill but inwardly seethe. Later the resentment came out in subtle but damaging ways.

19

Given my personality, I used to feel that peace at any price was the objective. I couldn't *stand* robust arguments, while my husband seemed to thoroughly enjoy them. I had the mistaken idea that it was "spiritual" to never express disagreements—that it was the "nice" thing to do. In our marriage we've come to realize that *when we are secure in each other's love, we have the freedom to express differences without threat.*

Often in a marriage where there is constant bickering, one needs to ask, "What's at stake here?" Maybe it's the question "Who's in charge?" Who determines what we spend our money on, what we do on Saturday, how we discipline our children, and who takes out the garbage? It's a power struggle. Who's going to win?

This major conflict provokes constant minor conflicts that will always be there until it's settled. In your marriage, who are you serving? There's no way a marriage can reach its full potential if each partner is out to please himself or herself first. Don't swallow the secular myth that you must be number one at all costs. You *are* a very important person, worth infinitely much in God's eyes, but this truth has been perverted to appeal to our basic selfish ego. "Self" is a deep hole. If one is constantly preoccupied with trying to fill it, it is never satisfied. The reverse is true: It is in giving that we receive.

Determine your basic conflict. Most marriage arguments involve sex, money, and family. Stand back and evaluate where you are struggling. Is there a basic sexual problem that you need to work through? Perhaps it is a lack of acceptance of the other person. Are you trying to make him something he is not? Is he doing that to you?

Resolve those conflicts. Why do you feel you "must win" in your marriage? Do you not feel important to your husband? If a conflict is never settled, it comes up again and again. Maybe it takes different forms, but it's the same conflict. "My husband went fishing, so I'll buy a dress." "He plays golf, so I'll go visit my mother." Perhaps the basic feeling of conflict is *"I don't feel I'm important to you or you'd spend more time with me."*

"My wife doesn't give me enough sex, so I'll make a derogatory remark about her in front of some friends." Tit for tat: It's an old-fashioned game of trying to get even. The sad thing is that in marriage, it doesn't work. Nobody wins. Going down the path of "getting even" is a good route to the divorce court. God created us to experience marriage as one flesh, and when we rip and tear our partner we are ripping and tearing ourselves.

It's important to work through these feelings of conflict. A conflict that is resolved brings two people closer together. There have been many times when Bill and I have talked things out long into the night. Each conflict that is worked through with forgiveness and acceptance brings a new depth of intimacy. You know each other a little more. You understand what is driving your partner, why he feels that way. Rolling over and letting things slide may be easier for the moment, but in the long run it doesn't solve anything.

Stand back and see the larger picture. Another word for unity is "harmony." You wouldn't enjoy listening to an orchestra where everyone played a different piece of music, but how often that is true of marriage! Each of us does our own thing. It isn't pleasant for our children to listen to this type of "music" we are creating for them. And we don't enjoy it ourselves, either. Put God in charge of your marriage. It was His idea in the first place! Your marriage is very sacred and very special to Him. It is an illustration of His love for us (Ephesians 5:21-33). We are to submit ourselves to each other in the fear of the Lord, knowing that ultimately He is our Lord. In other words, we need to recognize Him as the Master Conductor. We must submit our wills, our temperaments, our desires to Him—and then to each other.

Ask yourself some hard questions. What is important to you in your marriage? Are you really loving your husband? Do you give him the respect he desperately needs? Have you earned his respect? How do you express your disagreements?

There are ways to do this that are constructive and bring peace, unity, and understanding. We can "grow up" and learn to speak the truth in love (Ephesians 4:15). God has given us the will and the intelligence to *choose* our conversation: "A man hath joy by the answer of his mouth, and a word spoken in due season, how good is it!" (Proverbs 15:23).

RESOURCES

Love and Anger in Marriage. David Mace. Zondervan, 1982.
Close Companions: The Marriage Enrichment Handbook. David Mace. Continuum Publishing Co., 1982.
How to Express Anger. David Augsburger.
James 3.

NOTES

1. *My Side of the Story.* Ruth Bell Graham.

QUESTION 3

> ## *My husband doesn't feel my sexual response is adequate.*

Sexual problems in marriage are frustrating. Your basic desire is to love and be loved, to express warmth and tenderness and to enjoy sexual fulfillment. When this doesn't happen, a couple can be overwhelmed by a sense of failure, blame, or hostility. To not be desired by one's mate can produce the deepest feelings of rejection.

There are many reasons why couples do not respond sexually to each other. Research indicates that out of a whole week the average couple spends an hour or two in physical lovemaking. What happens the rest of the week obviously has some influence on the quality of your love life!

Perhaps you have some basic hangups about sex: Somehow you've gotten the impression that sex is not all it's cracked up to be, or that it's sinful. Possibly you've had a bad experience in your past that has influenced you.

Sometimes women who have many pressures with children, activities, and responsibilities can view sex as one more demand her husband is placing on her. Sex then becomes to her not a pleasure but another chore. She may feel "overloaded" and irritated with her husband's insensitivity.

Dr. Ed Wheat in *Love Life for Every Couple* (Zondervan, 1980) states, "...the entire lovemaking episode involves three phases of physical response that are interlocking but separate and easily distinguishable. There are desire, excitement, and orgasm.... Problems arise when an inhibiting 'switch' turns off any one of these physical responses in your

23

system.'' Dr. Wheat goes on to say that your sexual relationship is a reflection of the larger context of your life. For example, if you have deep hostilities toward your husband, your response will be limited.

First Corinthians 7:3-5 warns against defrauding each other in marriage—that is, withholding sex from each other except for mutually agreed to times of fasting and prayer. If a wife turns her husband down (or the reverse), she feels guilty, he feels rejected, and a vicious cycle begins. Perhaps the whole subject of sex in your marriage has become so emotionally charged that you can't be objective about it. You only know it's a sore subject.

The first thing you must realize is that *it is God's gift for you to have a fulfilling sex life.* Sex is *not* incidental and unimportant in marriage! It is not only for procreation. God has created us with the capacity to enjoy each other as husband and wife. We are different from animals in that we face each other when we have sexual contact. It is a wonderful means of communication. Hebrews 13:4 says, ''Marriage is honorable in all, and the bed undefiled.'' Sex is a gift from God to help us become one flesh (Genesis 2:24). Every time you have sexual intercourse with your husband, you are *nourishing the one flesh.* If you are having problems in this area, it is *vital* to your marriage to get some help!

In the secular view, women give sex to get love and men give love to get sex. Don't play these deadly games in marriage! I used to believe that *after* we got all our differences settled, *after* we communicated effectively, *after* Bill gave me roses and was sweet all week, then we would have a terrific love life. While you must settle differences, I've found that it is sometimes best to just open my arms and heart, and talk later. The problems that seem insurmountable before intercourse take on a completely different perspective later. If you can possibly do this, mentally take whatever is hindering you (inhibitions, whatever) and shelve them. Then set about enjoying your husband. What we are doing when we withhold sex because of our ''feelings'' is giving a conditional love, a please-me-or-pay attitude.

Talk to each other about your sex life! Cliff and Joyce Penner, in the September/October 1983 issue of *Virtue* magazine, recommend that a couple get a book and read it together. "We don't recommend professional help at first. The couple needs to start talking to each other, and a good way to start is to use a book. We often encourage couples to read our book aloud to each other because they will have the opportunity to say the sexual terms aloud and talk about sexual matters that they may have never discussed before. This is a more comfortable situation because they don't have to come up with all the sexual terms or anything else; all they have to do is read the book and discuss it.

"Discussion will happen much more spontaneously if they're reading to each other than if they read the book separately and then try to discuss it. If a couple find that they do in fact need professional help, they will have defined their problem much more clearly through discussion. Self-help is quite beneficial because the majority of people will not seek professional help. Many are in places where there isn't a trained professional. Also, many people will not go for counseling because of their inhibitions or financial limitations. . . .

"We feel strongly that one of the reasons that there is a lot of sexual dissatisfaction among women is that they don't take responsibility for themselves. Many women think that their husbands should instinctively know where they like to be touched, what will work and what won't work. People think you can learn how to relate sexually in three easy steps and that every woman is the same. It just isn't that way. People change from moment to moment, and needs vary from one person to another. The only way to be really satisfied is if a woman takes the responsibility to communicate to her husband what brings enjoyment at the moment, and then actively pursues that satisfaction."

As Dr. Wheat stated, *desire* is one of the most important elements in lovemaking. Whatever has gone into your past that has given you a bad attitude toward sex, *leave it* and concentrate on changing those attitudes. A wise older woman once shared in a Bible study, "The key to sex in marriage is mental! It all starts here," she told us younger women, tapping her head with her finger. I think she's right! I know one woman who was simply "turned off" by her husband's body odor. She solved that by getting him to shower with her before they went to bed! Ask the Lord for creativity to rekindle your desire for your husband. Then *talk to your husband.* Tell him what pleases you. When you are open with each other, you can experience the excitement and fulfillment that God intended for you to have.

RESOURCES

The Act of Marriage. Tim LaHaye and Beverly LaHaye. Zondervan, 1976.

The Gift of Sex. Clifford and Joyce Penner. Word Books, Inc., 1981.

Intended for Pleasure. Ed and Gaye Wheat. Fleming H. Revell, 1981.

$\mathcal{Q}$UESTION 4 _____

> ## *My husband wants me to perform sexual acts I think are wrong.*

Couples frequently do not agree on what constitutes acceptable sexual behavior between two married people. The actual sexual behaviors in question can run the gamut from mild differences in preferences to extreme or bizarre behavior.

Rather than discussing specific behaviors at this point, I think it would be more appropriate to discuss some principles.

First, let's talk about what is *not* acceptable under any circumstances.

1. *Sexual behavior of any kind that involves a person other than your spouse.* It is clear from God's Word that any sexual act with a person you are not married to, even with the consent or approval of your spouse, is wrong.

2. *Sexual behavior that is forced upon you against your will.* Sex in its proper function in marriage is two people giving their bodies to each other in an act of love and pleasure. It is in the very act of giving this pleasure that one receives pleasure. Therefore it stands to reason that performing sexual acts that are distasteful, unpleasurable, painful, or otherwise a negative experience to you or your spouse will not bring real pleasure to either party.

Furthermore, to perform acts against one partner's wishes is a violation of the trust which that person bestowed to you when the marriage vows were recited to "love, honor, and cherish."

3. *Withholding lovemaking from your marriage partner.* Touching, holding, caressing, and sexual intercourse should be a normal and regular part of every marriage. These basic "sexual acts" are a normal part of any healthy marriage relationship. If one of you cannot participate in normal sexual relations, professional counseling help should be consulted.

But the real question that many of you are asking goes deeper than what we have already said. Some of you are concerned about behavior such as oral sex or other deviations from sexual intercourse.

Here are some principles that I think will help willing couples to establish guidelines for sexual behavior in their marriage.

1. *Include God in your lovemaking.* By this we mean that your relationship to God and your expression of concern or anxiety should be discussed together with God in prayer. Remember that He is concerned about every part of your lives. He is the One who has created the marvelous gift of sex for us to enjoy, and He wants us to experience pleasure and oneness in each other.

Some people feel comfortable in talking to God about everything *except* their sex life. Some have the idea (usually from early upbringing) that all sexual behavior is sinful, or at least unspiritual. I still counsel some people who have the attitude that when they crawl under the covers to make love with their spouse, they hope God cannot see through the covers. This, of course, is an unhealthy attitude. Open up to God. He knows everything about you, and He created you to be a sexual being with wholesome physical needs and desires. Talk to God about your sexual needs, frustrations, anxieties, and inhibitions. Give Him thanks and rejoicing for the sexual pleasures you enjoy.

2. *Honor each other.* Paul tells us that "love does not demand its own way. It is not irritable or touchy. It does not hold grudges and will hardly even notice when others do it wrong" (1 Corinthians 13:5 TLB). Remember that if a certain sexual behavior is not in keeping with our spouse's

wishes, true love will honor our marriage partner by refraining from that behavior. We should never place our marriage partner in a position to need to justify his/her reluctance to perform certain sexual behaviors. It should be sufficient for him to simply express his wishes and for us to lovingly honor his wishes. When we apply this principle, our partner will begin to relax, and new vistas of sexual pleasure will begin to open up.

3. *Learn the joy of giving rather than receiving.* This principle can certainly be applied to giving each other pleasure in marriage. When we enter into lovemaking, our own pleasure is always heightened and enhanced when our spouse is receiving pleasure. The opposite is also true: When we are performing sexual acts that are unpleasurable, distasteful, or painful to our marriage partner, our own sexual pleasure is diminished.

4. *Be creative.* It is easy for us to fall into the world's "everybody's-doing-it" pattern. Certain sexual practices and behaviors have become widely known; we hear or read about them in books, movies, talk shows, etc. We somehow get the idea that our sex life is missing something if we are not living up to this standard of performance. Forget the world's pace! Be creative by mutually setting your own pace. Do what you have found to be mutually pleasurable in the frequency that the two of you feel most comfortable with.

Continue to lovingly explore the gift of sex with each other, but don't do it by some preconceived standard of performance or behavior. Recognize that the two of you are unique; your own creativity can guide and control your behavior. A good rule of thumb is to remember there is no "norm" in sexual preference or practice. Your marriage union is uniquely special and subject to its own creative level of pleasure and practice.

5. *Guard what you feed your mind.* Nothing will create more discontent in your marriage than reading pornographic literature describing fictitious people who are accomplishing some form of sexual feat beyond normal human potential.

X-rated movies will create lust, appetites of deviant behavior, and dissatisfaction with your marriage relationship. All of us have fantasies, but dwelling on fantasies of having sex with people other than our spouse will not only impair our relationship with our spouse, but it will eventually bring us to a temptation to act out our fantasies.

Someone has said, "What you feed your mind is what you are." Just as important as feeding our bodies wholesome food for proper nutrition, we need to feed our minds wholesome food to have healthy emotional lives.

Sexual fantasies in themselves are not wrong. They are a normal part of human behavior. But when you fantasize, fantasize about your husband or wife in a tender, loving, caring relationship. This is a healthy type of fantasy that will enhance your life together.

RESOURCES

Intended for Pleasure. Ed Wheat and Gaye Wheat. Fleming H. Revell, 1981.

The Gift of Sex. Clifford and Joyce Penner. Word, Books, 1981.

QUESTION 5

> ## *I believe that my husband is having an affair. What should I do?*

This has become an increasingly common problem discussed among the Christian community. Whether it has always been going on and is just now coming out in the open, or whether the incidence is actually increasing, is hard to say. When we published an article about the "Unmentionable Temptation" (adultery) in the March/April 1983 issue of *Virtue* magazine, we were amazed at the amount of mail we received from anonymous writers who either were having an affair themselves or else had husbands involved in an affair.

Rarely does an affair just "happen" in a marriage. Because it took some time for this to develop in your marriage, everything probably won't turn around for you overnight. *But there is a positive course of action you can take.*

Your first feelings are probably of panic, incredible rejection, and grief. Your panic and intense desire to want to hold things together may cause you to lose your self-respect and compromise what you know to be right.

Dr. James Dobson, in his timely book *Love Must Be Tough,* speaks specifically to the victim of a relationship where the partner has found someone new and is moving away from the marriage relationship. Dr. Dobson does an excellent job of articulating the problem and pointing to a solution. He documents the following scenario.[1]

1. Marital conflict typically involves one partner who cares a great deal about the relationship and the other who is much more independent and secure.

31

2. As a [marriage] begins to deteriorate, the vulnerable partner is inclined to panic. Characteristic responses include grieving, lashing out, begging, pleading, grabbing and holding; or the reaction may be just the opposite, involving appeasement and passivity.
3. While these reactions are natural and understandable, they are rarely successful in repairing the damage that has occurred. In fact, such reactions are usually counterproductive, destroying the relationship the threatened person is trying so desperately to preserve (p. 31).

Dr. Dobson goes on to discuss this problem when he states:

> It has been my observation that the lust for the forbidden fruit is often incidental to the real cause of marital decay. Long before any decision is made to "fool around" or walk out on a partner, something basic has begun to change in the relationship. Many books on this subject lay the blame on failure to communicate, but I disagree. The inability to talk to one another is a *symptom* of a deeper problem, but not the cause itself. The critical element is the way one spouse begins to perceive the other and their lives together. It is a subtle thing at first, often occurring without either partner being aware of the slippage. But as time passes, one individual begins to feel trapped. That's the key word, *trapped.*

Dr. Dobson subsequently tells us how probabilities are increased for the marriage to be saved:

> *The answer requires the vulnerable spouse to open the cage door and let the trapped partner out!* All the techniques of containment must end immediately, including manipulative grief, anger, guilt and appeasement. Begging, pleading, crying, hand-wringing and playing the role of the doormat are equally destructive. There may be a time and place for strong feelings to be expressed and there may be occasion for quiet tolerance. But these responses must not be used as persuasive devices to hold the drifting partner against his or her will (p. 45).

Dr. Dobson recognizes the iron determination and strong resolve it takes for one who is feeling all these overwhelming emotions of pain, guilt, and abandonment to stick to the plan and really "let go." However, it is his observation that this indeed offers the best chance of a change of heart and reconciliation. He states: "If the more vulnerable spouse passes the initial test and convinces the partner that his freedom is secure, some interesting changes begin to occur in their relationship. Please understand that every situation is unique and I am merely describing typical reactions, but these developments are extremely common in families I have seen. Three distinct consequences can be anticipated when a previously "grabby" lover begins to let go of the cool spouse:

1. The trapped partner no longer feels it necessary to fight off the other, and their relationship improves. It is not that the love affair is rekindled, necessarily, but the strain between the two partners is often eased.

2. As the cool spouse begins to feel free again, the question he has been asking himself changes. After having wondered for weeks or months, "How can I get out of this mess?" he now asks, "Do I really want to go?" Just knowing that he can have his way often makes him less anxious to achieve it. Sometimes it turns him around 180 degrees and brings him back home!

3. The third change occurs not in the mind of the cool spouse but in the mind of the vulnerable one. Incredibly, he feels better—somehow more in control of the situation. There is no greater agony than journeying through a vale of tears, waiting in vain for the phone to ring or for a miracle to occur. Instead, the person has begun to respect himself and receive small evidences of respect in return. Even though it is difficult to let go once and for all, there are ample rewards for doing so. One of these advantages involves feeling that he has a plan—a program—a definite course of action to follow. That is infinitely more comfortable than experiencing the utter

despair of powerlessness that he felt before. And little by little, the healing process begins."

We saw these principles work in the marriage of friends. The husband had a great amount of stress in his work, with financial and other considerations. He also was personally depressed at the way his business was going. At this vulnerable point in his life, enter a secretary—recently divorced after her husband had left her for another woman. She was extremely vulnerable as well. Before long there was a hot romance going, and the wife finally caught on to what was happening. He had always been a good provider to her and their three children, and she was devastated. The wife had the presence of mind (and self-respect) to calmly and firmly draw the line: "It's her or me." He chose the wife. This happened several years ago. Recently the wife confided, "It wasn't easy at first. I had to learn divine forgiveness! We went for marriage counseling that taught us both a lot about ourselves. But we're together, we're a family, and things are good."

We would counsel you to do three things at this critical point in your life.

1. *Take time for personal prayer and study of God's Word.* This will give you inner resources and strength you must have as you wade through this critical and confusing time. It's wonderful to have Christian friends who will pray with you and talk with you, but aside from that, find your own quiet time. "In returning and rest shall you be saved; in quietness and in confidence shall be your strength" (Isaiah 30:15).

2. *Find a competent Christian counselor who is also committed to having your marriage remain intact.* Too many counselors these days concentrate on "saving" the individual while the family disintegrates. I wonder what this actually does for the individual, not to mention the rest of the family!

3. *Get a copy of Dr. James Dobson's book,* **Love Must be Tough.** We thoroughly agree with Dr. Dobson's assessment

and urge you to get his book and read his entire counsel on the matter.

RESOURCES

Love Must Be Tough. James Dobson. Word Books, 1983.
The Myth of Greener Pastures. J. Allan Petersen. Tyndale.
Men and Mid-Life Crisis. Jim Conway. David C. Cook, 1978.
Hope for the Separated. Gary Chapman. Moody Press, 1982.

NOTES

1. *Love Must Be Tough.* James Dobson. Word Books, 1983.

QUESTION 6

> ## *My husband threatens or beats me. What should I do?*

First, we want to assure you that you are not alone in facing this awful problem. While wife-beating has no doubt always been with us, law enforcement agencies estimate that it touches a substantial number of families in today's society in one form or another.

There is no question any longer that men who beat or threaten to beat their wives have suffered severe emotional handicaps somewhere in their lives. Many men in our "macho" society have picked up the idea that dominating a woman physically is an acceptable form of behavior, or at least an excusable way to vent their frustrations. Television, movies, books, and other forms of propaganda have portrayed the desirable man as a violent man, capable of doing physical harm to other human beings. Women are frequently portrayed not as valuable human individuals but as playthings, sexual objects, or attachments to the man's ego and lifestyle. Men like this who resort to physical abuse need professional help.

I recognize that you are in a very serious dilemma of what to do. This man you married once declared his undying love and devotion to you. With marriage he became your closest friend, your love, and your confidante. He in essence became your "world." Now, when this same person turns from a beloved husband into a wife-beater, you have been plunged into a dilemma. The one who is supposed to be closest to you becomes the dreaded enemy of violence, and you are the victim. Exposing him may seem almost as difficult as letting the abuse go on. Many wife-beaters keep up a good facade. You may be looked on as an ideal or happily married couple. And your reputation and marriage are at stake. You have got a lot to lose if the marriage fails or other people discover the awful truth.

In addition, battered wives have the emotion of love for the man ("often he's kind and gentle" or "when he's sober he's beautiful to live with") mixed with rage and fear for his uncontrollable and unpredictable outbursts of violence. If there are children in the home, the dilemma of what to do becomes even more complex.

Here are some guidelines and resources that we hope will help point you in the right direction.

1. *Evaluate.* The first thing you must do is evaluate whether your husband is willing to seek professional help in overcoming this problem. Experts tell us that there are basically two types of wife-beaters—treatable and untreatable. "Treatable" wife-beaters are those who are normally in control of their emotions, but occasionally (or frequently) lose control and become violent with their wives. Afterward they are very guilt-ridden and remorseful. They feel the shame of what they have done, and vow to their wife that it will never happen again.

An "untreatable" wife-beater is the man who doesn't care. Violence is a part of his lifestyle, and he is abusive in many situations with a variety of people. He doesn't seek psychological counseling, and if he is somehow lured into a counseling situation, he will seldom act interested in changing his behavior.

2. *Get help.* If in your evaluation you feel your husband is treatable, then you should ask him to go with you for counseling. If your husband refuses to seek help, or if in your opinion he is untreatable, then for your personal safety and the safety of your children, you must seek help on your own. You should first confide in your pastor or select a good Christian counselor in your community. Often he will have

references or resources, possibly even a place to stay until the problem is resolved.

3. *Set a course of resolution.* As hard as it may seem to do, you must set a firm course of action. Just "letting it go this time" and hoping there is no "next time" is not sufficient. You have no doubt already noticed an all-too-familiar pattern. Often it is only after you have taken steps of action (such as moving out and going to stay with friends or relatives or in a shelter) that a husband is willing to seriously consider professional counseling.

4. *Take action.* It is not wise to be convinced by your husband of his good intentions without some action on his part to help overcome the problem. Often a husband will agree to get help only if you change your plan of action. But frequently, once the wife has decided not to go through with her plan of action, he goes back on his word to seek help. For this reason you should insist that he *go through a treatment/counseling program before you normalize the relationship again.* The degree of physical abuse that your husband resorts to may dictate the degree of action you decide to take. If it is severe verbal threats with an occasional slap, you may have more time to negotiate. However, if you have suffered physical beatings and you have reason to believe he may attack you again, you must remove yourself from the danger of the situation as soon as possible.

5. *Seek out a trusted Christian counselor.* You not only need the trust and support of someone who will listen to you, but you also need help in dealing with your emotions. The potential bitterness and resentment that can build up during these times can affect your health. All of the mixed emotions that you are struggling with need a sounding board. You also need the objective input of someone who can evaluate your situation from another perspective to help you decide exactly what course of action to take.

6. *Pray.* There is power in prayer. Your husband *can* change, or God can give you release and a new life if your husband continues to be unwilling to change. Never under-

estimate the power of God to transform something ugly into something beautiful. Prayer will also give you the "peace that passes understanding" (Philippians 4:7).

7. *Don't condemn yourself.* Many victims of wife abuse have been told by their husbands that they are stupid, uncaring, unworthy, terrible wives, and many battered wives believe what they hear.

It's true that all of us have faults and character flaws of one type or another. None of us is perfect. However, *nothing* you do (or don't do) deserves a beating from your husband. Other ways of resolving conflict in your marriage must be developed. Violence is never God's pattern in resolving conflicts in our interpersonal relationships!

Statistics show that men who develop a wife-beating pattern, when married a second or third time, often continue to beat their new wives. *It is not your fault,* and condemning yourself will not solve the problem.

Here are some additional ideas to help you plan a course of action.

1. *Normalize your life as much as possible.* Stop devoting all your energies to placating your husband. The task is impossible to accomplish. Instead, spend your time and energy helping your children, keeping the home environment as pleasant for you and the kids as possible. Help your children to be free from the negative influence of this problem by encouraging activities with wholesome families outside your home. Also, spend time drawing closer to God through prayer and study of God's Word. Immerse yourself in God's Word so that He can sustain you.

2. *Treat alcohol influence.* There is a debate as to whether some men drink in order to have an excuse to beat their wives ("I was drunk and didn't know what I was doing") or if in fact alcohol drives a man to beat his wife.

At any rate, if your husband consumes alcohol and if he has ever used this reason or excuse, or if you have observed heightened violent tendencies while drinking, treatment for alcoholism should be a part of his overall therapy.

3. *Make contingency plans.* If your decision is to stay in your home with your husband for now, try to confidentially arrange an emergency place for you to go in the event you must flee the conflict. Talk to your pastor, call a good shelter, or find a trusted friend who will let you come in an emergency. You may also want to plan ways of dealing with the next time. For example, if a familiar pattern develops (Friday nights after he's been out drinking), you may want to invite a friend to spend the night. Wife-beaters are usually very reluctant to perform their awful deeds in the presence of a third party.

4. *Learn independent skills.* This is not to suggest that you already plan to leave your husband for good. But independent skills could sustain you during the interim or make provision for you if you are cut off from financial support. In addition, it will insure your own personal self-worth. Your husband's respect for you may increase when he notices that you are capable of personal achievement and self-support.

RESOURCES

Child Help USA, telephone (800) 422-4453, keeps a listing of shelters for battered wives. While not every area has a shelter, many counties do have shelters.

Part II

Divorce

QUESTION 7

> **One of us wants out of this marriage.**
> **Can you give me some Biblical advice?**

Much is being written and debated about divorce today. The subject of divorce has become one of the most controversial issues in the church. Denominations, local churches, and individual Christians are all caught in the conflict over a correct Biblical position on this vital subject.

It would be impossible to put forth simple answers in a few words when many sensitive evangelical theologians, pastors, and counselors are struggling with the same problem. There are no easy solutions.

First, we must recognize that each marriage situation is unique, with its own set of dynamics and circumstances. One simply cannot apply pat answers that are universal. Each situation must be dealt with in the light of Scriptural teaching, obedience to what God is saying to us, our conscience, wise counsel from those spiritual leaders who are familiar with us, our emotional makeup and the emotional makeup of our spouse, and the particular circumstances that are unique to our situation.

The following is some advice, but it is only *general advice*. As already stated, because of the uniqueness of each marriage, you should seek the counsel of trusted spiritual leadership to help you through your marriage crisis.

1. *God's ideal.* Most of us would agree that God's ideal is for those who have entered into a marriage covenant to keep that covenant until "death do us part."

There is something to be said about commitment. In many

ways we Americans have lost the meaning of *commitment*. Not just marriage commitments suffer today, but the *principle of commitment* as well. It used to be that a person's word was as good as his signature and pledged assets. Entire reputations were at stake if people did not keep those commitments.

Today we have easy bankruptcy laws, easy divorce laws, and even "easy" commitments toward God and His principles.

While God's grace does indeed forgive us for *any* and *all* sin, it does not negate His expectation that we should continue to diligently strive for His ideal. After describing the wonderful forgiving grace of God, Paul asked, "Shall we go on sinning so that grace may increase?" His resounding answer was, "By no means!" (Romans 6:1,2 NIV).

Some of the strongest and most complete marriages I know have at one time gone through real crisis. In fact, there are very few marriages that have not gone through some rough places. All marriages need two people's dedication to commitment in their vows and pledged love toward each other in order to survive.

God's examples toward us in His covenants provide good examples for us to follow. In spite of our sin, in spite of our unfaithfulness, in spite of our inconsistency, in spite of our failures, God's love, acceptance, and forgiveness are never-failing, never-ending.

That's why we are told in Ephesians 5:22-25 to submit to each other and to love each other "as Christ loved the church and gave Himself for it."

My encouragement to you is that if there is *any* glimmer of hope or love left, however small or bleak, *keep trying to resolve the conflict, and allow God to work a miracle!*

God's ideal is for you to keep your marriage covenant. This may not always be pleasurable or easy. This does not always include the spark of romance and the euphoria of "love."

In fact, it may be painfully hard work with little or nothing in return for a long time. But that's what *commitment* is!

Paul pleads, "I beseech you therefore, brethren, by the mercies of God, that you present your bodies a living sacrifice, holy, acceptable unto God, which is your reasonable service. And be not conformed to this world, but be transformed by the renewing of your mind, that you may prove what is that good, and acceptable, and perfect, will of God" (Romans 12:1,2).

2. *Bitterness and unforgiveness.* Occasionally one hears of two people who dissolved their marriage yet remained good friends, with little or no blame, resentment, or hostility by either party. However, this is the exception, not the rule. Most marriage problems and subsequent breakups carry with them deep hurts, resentments, unforgiveness, and feelings of bitterness.

The one basic foundation of our faith is forgiveness. Without God's promise of complete forgiveness, we simply have no basis for our Christian faith. God not only set the example and pattern of forgiveness, but He frequently tells us to follow that pattern. In Jesus' own example of effective prayer He states, "Forgive us our debts, as we forgive our debtors" (Matthew 6:12). Here are some other Scriptures that leave no doubt as to God's expectations on this issue of forgiveness.

Matthew 6:14,15: "For if you forgive men their trespasses, your heavenly Father will also forgive you; but if you forgive not men their trespasses, neither will your Father forgive your trespasses."

Ephesians 4:32: "Be kind one to another, tenderhearted, forgiving one another, even as God for Christ's sake has forgiven you."

Forgiveness is expected by God not only in the marriage relationship, but in *all* relationships. Harboring anger, resentment, bitterness, or any offense committed against us is a sin equal to the offenses originally committed. In marriage especially, the unresolved offenses and negative patterns that have built up over the years—all the hurtful words, all the acts of infidelity, and all the lies and inconsistencies—simply must be forgiven if your life is ever to be blessed by God.

Whether or not your marriage is ultimately dissolved, and whether you are the perpetrator or the victim of divorce, you must ask God to help you genuinely forgive your spouse for the hurts of the past. You can never be happy or blessed by God without first giving forgiveness to your spouse.

Here are some other questions to ask yourself if you are the one contemplating the divorce.

1. *Have I given God and this marriage every possible chance to survive?* You are not ready to contemplate divorce until all other avenues have been totally and completely exhausted.

2. *Is there someone else of the opposite sex in my life who is meeting some or all of my emotional needs?* If so, you are not in a position to give your marriage every chance to survive or even to have a rational head and heart to make proper decisions. Another person of the opposite sex who has in any way taken the place of your marriage partner (emotional intimacy, spiritual intimacy, physical intimacy, or a combination of all three) will cloud your vision and ability to reason. Seek counseling to resolve this dangerous relationship before you move on to solve your own marriage problems.

3. *How will this affect other people?* You must weigh the consequences of how a divorce will affect the lives of others. Consider your children: How will it impair their overall development as well as their future perception and expectations? Never fool yourself into believing that it will not affect them—it will! How will the sticky issue of custody and visitation rights be played out in their lives over the next five to ten years? What about your parents, your in-laws, the people in your church, your friends, your pastor? How many people will be affected by your decision, and how will it affect them? We must remember that a divorce, no matter how "smooth," is a ragged, tearing-apart of a family unit,

a unit built over the years with relationships, kinfolk, friends, children, grandparents, and church family.

4. *Has God given me complete and total release from this marriage?* If you cannot answer this question with a positive yes, then you need to *wait.* Wait for God, wait on God, wait to see how God works in this situation. Isaiah said, "Those who wait upon the Lord shall renew their strength; they shall mount up with wings as eagles; they shall run and not be weary; they shall walk and not faint" (Isaiah 40:31).

RESOURCES

Why Christian Marriages Are Breaking Up. Gerald L. Dahl. Thomas Nelson Publishers, 1981.

Strike the Original Match. Chuck Swindoll. Multnomah Press, 1980.

QUESTION 8

How does divorce affect children?

Although neither of us has experienced divorce firsthand, we do have close friends who have divorced. We have walked with them and cried with them as their lives were shredded apart. We have counseled people going through divorce. Nobody *likes* divorce. It just seems to be a human solution to an unworkable marriage.

The more I read about children of divorce and listen to children of divorce, the more convinced I am that *they* are the real victims of divorce. Their whole world is dismantled, and they have nothing to say about it. To make it even more traumatic, parents can't be of much help to their children during this most stressful time because they are so torn up themselves.

Divorce in a Christian family has an added complication. Often children pray to have their parents come back together—and their prayers aren't answered. My mother babysat a six-year-old girl whose parents were divorcing. Much bitterness was involved. The little girl prayed every night, "God, *please* bring my daddy home." Due to the personal choices of the parents, God could not answer that prayer! A child whose parents are going through divorce will wonder if his parents are really Christians. If they are, why couldn't they work out their problems? Why didn't God stop this?

If you have children and are contemplating divorce, I would urge you to consider all the ramifications *carefully*.

Pat Chavez, author of *Picking Up the Pieces*, urges, "Exhaust all possibilities. If you have any choice at all, *don't divorce.*" Archibald D. Hart, author of *Children and Divorce*, says:

> Since divorcing parents often—if not always—feel guilty about what they are doing, they gratefully accept the placating platitudes of friends who say, "The kids will get over it; it's amazing how resilient they are," or "Divorce is not a catastrophe for children; they will survive it." This is not helpful.
>
> While I do not want to create problems where none exist, I do believe it is time we more realistically evaluated the consequences of divorce on children. . . .[1]

Dr. Lee Salk, prominent child psychologist, says, "The trauma of divorce is second only to death. Children sense a deep loss and feel they are suddenly vulnerable to forces beyond their control."

If you are in an abusive situation and feel you must make some immediate changes for the sake of the children and yourself, do so. Separate—but get good counsel and proceed carefully. If your husband is having an affair with another woman, it is of course an intolerable situation. *But your marriage can still be salvaged.* If you are in this kind of situation, read Dr. James Dobson's book *Love Must Be Tough.* He offers excellent counsel that really works.

It is also possible that your marriage is over, and that there's nothing you can do about it. It takes two to make a marriage work. Perhaps the divorce was not your choice at all, and you are left to pick up the pieces. Remember, we have a big God who offers forgiveness, healing, and restoration.

Parents will often use the argument that a divorce is better for the children because of the parents' fighting. The children evidently don't share that view. In a survey asked of children of divorce, less than 10 percent report being relieved by their parents' divorce. Children of divorce fantasize about their parents getting back together.

Here are some of the vulnerabilities to divorce of each age group of children.

Toddlers (ages 2-4):   Regression in their behavior; becoming "babyish." Some psychologists feel that the absence of the parent of opposite sex may be detrimental to the child's sexual development.

Young children (ages 5-8):   Also regression. They often take responsibility for the breakup; have irrational fears of abandonment, sleep problems, bedwetting, and nail-biting; have a deep sense of sadness; retreat into fantasy as a way of solving the family crisis.

Older children (ages 9-12):   Anger; anger directed at a parent; grief. The child may alienate those close to him. Spiritual development is easily damaged at this age by disappointment and disillusionment.

Teenagers: Deep hurt and resentfulness. Teenagers fear being separated from their friends and become depressed. They feel torn emotionally by trying to keep peace with both parents.

Although this is a painful time for you personally, concentrate on what your child is feeling. Children often blame themselves for their parents' breakup, even though they don't verbalize it. The two people most important in your child's life are now at two separate addresses—and he's in the middle. Talk to your child. Many children deal with their pain by silence, but they need to talk about it. They must know that they are not the cause of the divorce. Pat Chavez, a director of Divorced Recovery Workshops, offers these important points for parents to consider.

In telling the children about the divorce:
Be sure to tell them personally.
Be quick to explain that it's not their fault.
Don't make children choose where they live. You and the children's father make that decision for them.
In determining custody of the children:
Try to separate *your* needs for the children from *their* needs.

> Remember, your child still needs both parents.
>
> Determine which living environment is best for the child.
>
> Disrupt a child's sense of security as little as possible.
>
> Try to establish joint custody, unless one parent is abusive, or custody for one parent with unlimited visitation for the other.[2]

In other words, though it may be extremely difficult for you to be objective, *put your children's welfare above your own.* You may wish to never "see the louse again," but he *is* your children's father. Resist the temptation to be critical of him in front of your child. Don't allow anyone else to criticize him in front of your children either. You will only alienate your children if you let them see your personal bitterness against their father.

As with any child going through a grief process, your child needs a lot of hugging, touching, and verbal assurances of love. It's okay to cry with your child! Read the excellent book *What Children Need to Know When Parents Get Divorced*, by William L. Coleman. This book is geared to children aged 6-12. If you are finding it difficult to talk to your children about the divorce, perhaps reading this book to them will open the door.

Family is important at this time. If your children's grandparents are close by, or other relatives, perhaps they can visit with them occasionally, helping them feel "special" and that they still do have a family.

By being loving and patient with your child, you can help him regain his hope for the future. Help him see that just because his parents are divorcing *each other* does not mean that they will be divorcing *him.* Your own example of wholehearted trust in God will influence his own ability to trust God even in this hard time.

One pastor's wife who experienced a devastating and totally unexpected divorce tells how she and her three sons sat and prayed and talked for hours following the breakup. She felt very close to her sons during the immediate crisis time, and together they worked out their grief. It was rough, but they were able to keep their faith stubbornly fixed on God, and eventually could offer forgiveness to her husband.

One caution: Be careful not to make your child a "surrogate" spouse, thus placing emotional demands on him that he cannot fulfill. In other words, remember that he is still your child, and you are his parent.

RESOURCES

Children and Divorce. Archibald D. Hart. Word, 1982.
Picking Up the Pieces. Patricia Chavez and Clif Cartland. Thomas Nelson Publishers, 1979.
What Children Need to Know When Parents Get Divorced. William L. Coleman. Bethany Fellowship, 1983.

NOTES

1. *Children and Divorce.* Archibald D. Hart. Word Books, 1982.
2. *Picking Up the Pieces.* Patricia Chavez and Clif Cartland. Thomas Nelson Publishers, 1979.

QUESTION 9

> **The divorce is final and I'm hurting.
> How can I put the pieces back together?**

Divorce is a deep emotional crisis. As in a death, there is a deep scar of loss accompanied by grief. It is pain-filled and traumatic, but it is not the end of your world. Contrary to what you may be feeling now, there is hope, there is life, there is a future for you.

Here are some concepts that will help you cope now and soon begin to put the pieces of your life back together again.

1. *Release it to God.* You are not alone in this situation. You may feel lonely, forsaken, and unloved, but Jesus is with you. It was Jesus Himself who said, "I will *never* leave you or forsake you" (Hebrews 13:5). In another verse He tells us, "Peace I leave with you; my peace I give unto you; not as the world gives, give I unto you. Let not your heart be troubled, neither let it be afraid" (John 14:27).

While you may be frightened, confused, or angry, God promises that if you trust in Him with all your heart, lean not on your own understanding, and acknowledge Him in all your ways, He *will* direct your paths (Proverbs 3:5,6).

Remember also that you are not the first person to go through this crisis. Many others have experienced the shock, depression, and remorse you are now feeling. The church family is becoming more and more aware of those who have faced the trauma of divorce. In your community there are probably Christian single-adult groups that meet regularly in at least one church. There are probably also some divorce-recovery groups that meet regularly. Check with your pastor, your doctor, a trusted counselor, a local college, or a health agency to see if a divorce-recovery group counseling session is available.

The reason I suggest divorce-recovery groups is that the still-married society (even within the church) still does not always know how to reach out to divorced people. It is easier for them to respond to death in the family, cancer surgery, or fire destroying a house. For these things people bring food and tender concern, send flowers, and make loving phone calls of sympathy, but a divorce brings no such condolence in our society.

Be careful not to fault people for this, but to recognize it as a cultural blindness. Fear of "taking sides," a perception of failure, and feelings of awkwardness all contribute to the still-married society's lack of understanding.

But you can find those who will understand!

2. *Go ahead and mourn.* A period of mourning is a natural part of the loss you feel. All the emotions of separation, shock, loss, loneliness, remorse, and tears—lots of tears— are normal responses. Give vent to these and allow yourself time to mourn. Like a death, there has been a traumatic loss in your life. The mourning process will help you let go and eventually promote healing.

During this time you may also experience other emotions toward your former spouse, such as anger, bitterness, guilt, self-pity, listlessness, meaninglessness in life, embarrassment, and humiliation. These too are normal, and you should not condemn yourself for them. Talk to someone about these feelings—a pastor, trusted friend, or counselor—so that he or she can help you understand these feelings. This way you will eventually be able to overcome them. Ask God to release you from these feelings and to replace them with His joy and peace.

When is enough mourning? Psychologists and marriage counselors suggest that the mourning period usually lasts about six months. You can begin to tell for yourself when the mourning time has started to subside when all of these "feelings" no longer consume you, and you begin to feel that you will live through the divorce. You will begin to see your attitude improve, and you will begin to look to the future rather than continually dwelling on the past.

While mourning is important, it is also important to finish grieving and get on with your life. It is my opinion that if at first you give vent to all your feelings and let the tears flow, you will recover more quickly to get on with the rest of your life.

3. *Learn to forgive.* We dealt with this more specifically in Question 7. We encourage you to read the section on "Bitterness" (Question 11) to get a full picture on how you can forgive your spouse and be released.

Let me add that if you do not forgive, you can never totally "let go" and be released. Sometimes it requires another letter or conversation with your former spouse granting him or her total and unconditional forgiveness. Believe me when I say that this does as much (or more) for you as it does for him!

Otherwise the wound in your heart will eventually scab over and heal with scar tissue, but the wound will still be there, under the surface. The wound will have a tendency to resurface in other ways, affecting your relationship with more than just your ex-spouse. Bitterness and unforgiveness have a way of expressing themselves in bizarre ways...in our physical and/or mental health, in our behavior toward our children, or in other future relationships.

Whatever it takes, give and receive forgiveness so that you can be released to laugh, love, and grow again.

4. *Make friends with yourself.* Self-condemnation, personal guilt for failure, and self-pity will keep you from full recovery.

Yes, it takes two people to end a marriage. Yes, you no doubt could have acted differently in certain situations. Admit your fault and mistakes, seek forgiveness, ask God to separate the wrong "as far as the east is from the west," and go on with life. Dwelling in remorse, self-condemnation, and pity will eventually cause other people to avoid you (even your kids). It is like a poison.

Instead, dwell on your good points and begin to cultivate the positive qualities that you and others recognize in your life. Read a new book on the hobby you have wanted to start, take a class, invite some friends for dinner, buy some new clothes, invite a friend to lunch, or take your kids on a picnic. See yourself for the valuable, caring, sensitive, multitalented person that you can be. If Jesus has decided to call you a friend (John 15:15), then you should certainly stop condemning yourself for a failed marriage and start befriending yourself again!

5. *Get on with life.* Now is the time to set some new goals, make some plans. Consider what you want to do both short-range and long-range. Make some plans, be alive, get excited about your future. Develop some new interests and activities. If you have been thrown into the work force for the first time in several years, analyze your job. If it's temporary and you don't enjoy it, plan something more.

Decide what you want to do and how much education or training it will take, then devise a plan on how to get there.

6. *Remember that your kids are people too.* If you have custody of the children, there may be a strong tendency to put your entire emotional future and social interest in your children. This is not a healthy thing to do.

While all children need parental attention, when a child senses that a parent's emotional needs are his responsibility, he begins to feel crowded and trapped. While he loves you, he will resent being held responsible for your emotional happiness. He wants the freedom to grow up, to develop new relationships, to not feel guilty when his parent is no longer the center of his universe.

Overindulgence, overdependence, and overidentification with your children, their lifestyle, and their peers will have a tendency to drive them away from you—just the opposite response that you are hoping for.

Let them develop normal relationships while you as a parent develop normal relationships, so that together you give each other the freedom to live *with* each other, but not *for* each other. As you treat your kids like people (instead of objects of emotional dependence and your link to happiness), you will develop a long and lasting friendship with them.

If their independence is not threatened, they will come back to you for friendship, love, counsel, and sharing for the rest of their lives.

7. *Develop a new relationship. . . slowly.* Statistics indicate that second marriages have as much as a 50 percent higher divorce rate than first marriages!

Until you are fully emotionally recovered from your divorce, you are not in a position to get deeply involved in a new relationship. Jumping into a new relationship too quickly is the primary reason why second marriages frequently fail.

It is all too early, in our state of loneliness, to find someone quickly to fill the void. Often this new high feels so much better than the old pain and feelings of humiliation that it is difficult, if not impossible, to rationally determine whether this is God's choice for your life.

Here are three questions you need to ask yourself.

Is there any chance for reconciliation (remarriage) with my former spouse? Is he/she remarried? Can God still work in our lives? Could the marriage ever be revived? Many couples have remarried with great success. Remember that it is God's ideal for us to finish this life with our original commitments whenever possible.

Do I have control of my emotions? Am I still angry, bitter, or hurting over the divorce? Am I suffering bouts of loneliness and low self-esteem? Am I feeling like half a person without a spouse?

Does God want me to remain single? Many Scriptures refer to remaining single. In 1 Corinthians 7 Paul states a case for singlehood, especially after a person has been separated from his or her former spouse by divorce or death. While it is not commanded that the innocent party of a divorce remain single, it is pointed out as an option that should be prayerfully considered.

Depending on how you answer these questions, caution is in order for you in developing a new relationship.

A new relationship must be built on mutual love, respect, awareness, spiritual oneness, mutual considerations, and God's will. . . *not on emotional needs based on past feelings or failures!*

Jumping into another relationship just to satisfy emotional needs is a *sure* formula for failure. Be cautious. . . go slowly.

8. *View your divorce as an opportunity for growth.* Your life at the point of divorce is like a snow-covered patch of ground: cold and frozen, without much sign of life. You feel the gray, the shadows, and the cold.

But remember that spring is just around the corner, and that under the snow and frozen ground are seeds ready to blossom into life again. Now is the time to dig deep into God's Word. Read the Psalms; hide little treasures of Scripture in your heart like planted seeds.

This is an excellent time to let your aloneness become a source of spiritual depth and strength. Let prayer, meditation, reflection, and conversation with Jesus become an all-important part of your life. If you do, you will begin to feel strength and warmth come back into your life, and one day soon you will realize that spring and summer with their warmth and sunshine have returned to your life again!

RESOURCES

Prescription for a Broken Heart. Bobbie Reed. Regal Books, 1982.
Beyond Divorce: A Personal Journey. Brenda Hunter. Fleming H. Revell, 1978.
The Other Side of Divorce. Helen Hosier. Abingdon, 1980.
Growing Through Divorce. Jim Smoke. Harvest House Publishers, 1976.

Part III

Emotions

QUESTION 10

> **I'm experiencing terrible fear. Please help me.**

Fear can be one of the most debilitating and disruptive forces in our lives. Not only does it have the potential of handicapping our emotional well-being and our ability to make sound decisions, but prolonged fear can have a negative effect on our physical health. In fact, some medical science studies indicate that more than half of the patients consulting a physician have no organic disease. Rather, their symptoms are caused by tension, stress, worry, and depression—all the emotions associated with negative thinking and fear.

Doctors at the Mayo Clinic have said that 80 percent of the stomach disorders that come to their attention are not organic disorders but functional disorders caused by worry attitudes that affect the nervous system. Dr. Charles Mayo himself said that prolonged fear or worry affects the circulation, the heart, the glands, and the entire nervous system. "I have never known a man to die from overwork," said Dr. Mayo, "but many who have died from doubt."

Some fear is natural and beneficial. A child's fear of a busy street or of strangers (who may want to pick him up) is healthy. A doctor's fear of infection or a mother's fear for her two-year-old child near a deep body of water are types of healthy and normal "fears." The Bible tells us that "the fear of the Lord is the beginning of knowledge" (Proverbs 1:7). This kind of fear could be termed *respect*.

But fears of the unknown haunt us and profoundly affect our ability to function.

Not long ago an elderly woman who lived in occupied Europe during the Second World War spoke to us about her fear. She told us that ever since the horror of the war—the bombing raids, the death and dying, and the constant fear that she would be killed—she had been unable to sleep well at night. "Even now every night," she stated, "I wake up in a cold sweat with a terrible fear that the air raids will start again." For 40 years this woman has suffered this debilitating fear! It has affected her sleep patterns, her health, and her ability to have a normal life.

Fear and anxiety appear in many forms: fear of failure, fear of death or disease, fear of the unknown, fear of rejection, fear of other people's opinions of us, fear of financial ruin, or fear of an inability to provide for our families.

A look at Scripture quickly shows that God has a lot to say about fear: He does not intend for His children to live in fear. Second Timothy 1:7 says, "For God has not given us a spirit of fear, but of power and of love and of a sound mind." Jesus told His disciples, "Let not your heart be troubled, neither let it be afraid" (John 14:27).

Here are some specific keys to overcoming fear.

1. *Learn to discipline your thought life.* The apostle Paul on several occasions refers to how we think and what we think about. In Philippians 4:7 he makes this encouraging statement: "The peace of God, which passes all understanding, shall keep your hearts and minds through Christ Jesus."

In the next verse he says, "Whatsoever things are true, whatsoever things are honest, whatsoever things are just, whatsoever things are of good report—if there be any virtue, and if there be any praise, think on these things." Too often we feed our minds on untruth, unjust things, impure thoughts, unlovely ideas, and bad reports.

Someone has said, "What you feed your mind is what you are." Just as we should feed our bodies nutritious food rather than junk food, we need to feed our minds good, nutritious thoughts.

There is no constructive purpose in worrying about things that may never happen. That kind of worry will only do you harm. Someone has said, "God grant me the serenity to accept the things I cannot change, the courage to change the things I can, and the wisdom to know the difference."

You cannot change the future. You cannot avoid the unknown. Learn to trust God to provide divine guidance for you. Proverbs 3:5,6 states, "Trust in the Lord with all your heart, and lean not on your own understanding. In all your ways acknowledge him, and he shall direct your paths." That's good advice!

2. *Learn to discipline what you say.* Words are creative. The old saying "Sticks and stones may break my bones, but words can never hurt me" is simply not true. Our words can create good or evil both within ourselves and within other people. If a child is constantly told, "You are a bad boy," or a father repeatedly tells his teenager, "You'll never amount to anything," those words create attitudes which eventually will show up in the child's behavior pattern.

If we are critical, backbiting, and prone to gossip, our words will have a significant effect toward those about whom we are critical and gossiping. It will also ingrain a critical, bitter spirit within us.

If we speak words of praise, value, and dignity toward other people, we will not only have many friends who enjoy being around us, but we will see our words of encouragement and praise actively create good things in the lives of those around us as well as in ourselves.

The Psalmist said, "Set a watch, O Lord, before my mouth; keep the door of my lips" (Psalm 141:3). Jesus said, "Out of the abundance of the heart the mouth speaks" (Matthew 12:34). Learning to control what you say will be a big step in learning to control your thoughts. If you speak good words you will create circumstances and an environment for good things to happen in your life and in the lives of other people.

3. *Learn to act on the good thoughts you think and the good words you say.* After awhile this will become an automatic response because you become what you feed your mind. But at first you will need to *consciously act* on your new thought patterns and words. Begin to treat yourself and other people as really valuable gifts from God. Take action on the good thoughts and words. Make decisions on the positive potential rather than the negative possibilities.

4. *Learn to trust God.* We are not advocating some new mental game for you to play that says mind power will make you succeed. All we have said is rooted in a profound trust and faith in God. Recognize that freedom from fear is God's idea and plan. The Word of God is filled with encouragement in this area. Read Psalm 23, as well as such promises as 2 Timothy 1:7: "For God has not given us the spirit of fear, but of power and of love and of a sound mind." Also read Hebrews 13:5: "I will never leave you nor forsake you." If God's Word is true, then we have every assurance that we can live happy, productive lives through faith in His promises.

5. *Make God's will your will.* The constant temptation we all face is to fall back on our own logic, our own plans, our own reasoning, our own abilities. Recognize that this is the very thing that creates and reinforces fears and worry. Making *God's* will *our* will is an act of obedience. It involves quickly responding to the prompting of the Holy Spirit and quickly obeying God's voice. God speaks to us in many ways: through His word, through the counsel of a godly friend or leader, through our conscience, through circumstances, etc. The important thing is to *obey.*

When we recognize that God's plan is the best plan for us, and are quick to obey Him in that plan, we will discover a release from fear and a whole new world of joy and peace.

RESOURCES

Calm Down. Gary Collins. Christian Herald Books, 1981.
Emotions: Can You Trust Them? James Dobson. Regal Books,
1980.
Living Without Fear. Wilma Burton. Good News Publishers,
1981.

QUESTION 11

How can I overcome bitterness?

Bitterness stems from offenses (either real or perceived) that we hold inside ourselves; we blame someone else for some circumstance in our lives. When an offense is held in our hearts and minds long enough, it becomes resentment and a form of hatred that brings bitterness to our lives. Bitterness is not talked about very much. In our research we found very little on this subject even among psychologists. The reason may be that outside of Christian teachings, there really is no solution to bitterness.

It is only by faith in Jesus Christ and by using the power of the Holy Spirit that we can be healed of the deep roots of bitterness. I personally feel that bitterness is one of the most destructive emotions a person can experience.

Bitterness, when left unchecked, can caused serious physical, emotional, and spiritual problems. "See to it that no one fails to obtain the grace of God, that no root of bitterness springs up and causes trouble, and by it many become defiled" (Hebrews 12:15). Medical experts tell us that a significant percentage of illness in America is caused by psychological and emotional factors rather than by physiological factors. T.H. Holmes and R.H. Rane developed a "Social Readjustment Rating Scale" published in the *Journal of Psychosomatic Research*. The purpose was to measure the stress factors that people experience when going through certain types of readjustment. Stress is one of the major factors in heart attacks, stomach disorders, and a number of other diseases in America.

It is significant to note the top ten crises on the Social Readjustment Scale.

1. Death of a spouse
2. Divorce
3. Marital separation
4. Prison term
5. Death of a close family member
6. Personal injury or illness
7. Marriage
8. Fired from job
9. Marital reconciliation
10. Retirement

Notice how many of these involve broken relationships (divorce, separation, employment terminated), along with a prison term (crime is often caused by one's bitterness or anger toward someone else). I believe that in most cases these crises involve unresolved bitterness and resentment.

The irony of bitterness and resentment is that it winds up hurting the bitter person the most! Not only can it cause serious problems, but it affects us spiritually and emotionally as well. Scripture teaches that unforgiveness is the one poison that will hinder our progress and prevent God from giving us full forgiveness: "For if you forgive men their trespasses, your heavenly Father also will forgive you; but if you do not forgive men their trespasses, neither will your Father forgive your trespasses" (Matthew 6:14,15).

Here are some things you should consider to help resolve bitterness.

1. *Stop feeding your bitterness.* Our memory is a wonderful gift from the Lord; with it we recall all the warm and wonderful happenings of life. We also remember and learn from past mistakes. Unfortunately, we can also turn our memory into an ally for bitterness. Our minds have an incredible ability to remember and rehash offenses. Psychotherapists tell us that people cling to their bitterness to the

bitter end. "It's one of the most difficult things to deal with."

However, you can choose to rid yourself of bitterness if you really desire to. The first step is to *stop feeding it.* When you are tempted again to dwell on the offense, to dredge up the ugly past, to feel the resentment and to feed on the hate, choose instead to *starve* your bitterness by refusing to relive all the old hurts. Substitute your thought patterns with positive thoughts about other people whom you love and respect.

While you may not be able to instantly forget your bitterness, you can recognize that it is not the whole of your world. View this experience as an opportunity to learn patience, forgiveness, and a new depth of love. Recognize that God gave *everything* to you to reconcile you and restore you. Scripture tells us that we deserved death but have been wonderfully pardoned by God. Can we do less for those who have sinned against us?

2. *Stop keeping score.* Bitterness quickly becomes exaggerated when we begin to "keep score" and pile up new perceived offenses and incidents. Our "lawyer" mind shouts to build a case. Soon *everything* this person does starts to be offensive to us! This only adds to our bitterness.

3. *Stop justifying your bitter feelings.* The human psyche can come up with very elaborate excuses for hanging onto bitterness. That is because we want to hang onto it! Recognize that God offers no excuse for harboring bitterness, resentment, or unforgiveness. Simply put, we *must forgive.* It is not an option to the Christian.

Part of the risk of *loving greatly* is being *hurt greatly.* If we didn't care so much in the first place, we wouldn't be hurting so much. Bitterness is often love gone sour.

In our human relationships, we need to learn to love with an open-ended kind of love—the same kind of love that God showed us when He sent Jesus, His precious Gift, to the world. "He came to His own, and His own did not receive Him. But as many as received Him, to them He gave the right to become children of God, even to those who believe in His name" (John 1:11,12 NKJV).

If our love is not received, or is misunderstood, we must *redirect it*—keep sending, keep loving. Otherwise we become shriveled and atrophied.

Here are some positive steps to overcoming bitterness.

1. *Start forgiving.* While nothing is more harmful to us than bitterness and unforgiveness, nothing is more liberating than forgiveness. Forgiveness is a gift that God has given us so that we can give it to others. In so doing we give it back to ourselves. Forgiveness is an investment in our happiness and future, for as we forgive others, we become forgiven. Forgiveness will result in a reduction of tension and stress, a better chance to be healthy, and an inner peace and joy.

2. *Start turning your resentment into kindness.* Jesus gave us the instruction to "love your enemies, bless them that persecute you, do good to them that hate you" (Matthew 5:44). Psychologists confirm this principle by telling us that an important step to health is acting out our beliefs to strengthen our beliefs. Dr. Archibald D. Hart tells us that when we turn resentment into kindness, "it reinforces our belief system by giving us the feeling that we are in control. It protects us from our own anger and hostility."

3. *Start giving your feelings to God.* With God's help you can overcome bitterness. God is in the business of forgiving all your iniquities, healing all your diseases, and redeeming your life from destruction (Psalm 103). Every time you are tempted to dwell on your bitterness, give it over to God. Let it be an occasion to force you to pray and to dwell on the good things of life.

RESOURCES

Forgive, Forget and Be Free. Jeanette Lockerbie. Christian Herald Books, 1981.

It Feels Good to Forgive. Helen Hosier. Harvest House Publishers, 1980.

QUESTION 12

> ## I've become increasingly depressed. Is there a way out?

Jane started feeling down most of the time. Something inside her disturbed her, but she couldn't understand what it was. She found herself crying more, but for no specific reason. Jane's sleep pattern changed. She would wake up in the night and not be able to go back to sleep. Everything on the surface seemed to be okay—her family routine was normal and she wasn't physically ill except for frequent headaches (which was normal for her). Lately her spiritual life seemed bland and meaningless. She knew something was wrong, out of sync. Her appetite changed and she felt blue. Life was not fun anymore.

Jane was suffering what millions of Americans suffer. . . *depression.* Mental health experts tell us that nearly 75 million people suffer mild to moderate depression every year.

Christians are not exempt. Some well-meaning Christians try to promote the idea that Christians never have problems:

> "Look happy, act happy, be happy."
> "Pray about it. . . just give your problem to God and smile."
> "If you feel that way, there's got to be sin in your life—get rid of it."

Certainly prayer, repentance, and forgiveness are wonderful tools from the Lord and can indeed lead us to overcoming depression. Too often, however, well-meaning Christians

70

offer their "quick-fix" answers to a far deeper problem.

Dr. Timothy Foster, Christian psychologist and author of *How to Deal with Depression,* states, "The tendency to spiritualize depression is probably well intended, but is still unloving, judgmental and wrong." Other well-meaning Christians can put guilt on the depressed person by implying that good Christians never get depressed. But Christians have emotions too. And when their emotions become suppressed, depression will occur.

If you or someone you know is suffering from some or all of the symptoms described in Jane's case at the beginning of this chapter, it is probably depression.

The following are some specific symptoms to look for. Taken alone, these symptoms may not signal depression, although any one of them could be an early warning sign. Collectively, however, they give a good indication that you may be suffering from depression.

1. *The blues.* Sometimes you feel sad for no specific reason. Other times you don't really feel anything. You sense loneliness and distance from other people. You just feel blue. Often your emotions feel numb or you just don't care about things anymore. Prolonged "blue" feelings are a strong symptom of depression.

2. *Changed sleeping and eating habits.* When depressed, some people cannot sleep well, wake up in the night, and are not able to go back to sleep. Others may want to sleep all the time. After eight hours of sleep they wake up still feeling tired or sleepy. Another symptom of depression can be a notable increase or decrease in appetite. Any change in sleeping or eating habits and patterns can be a sign of depression.

3. *Emotional changes.* If you normally cry easily but now your crying has stopped, or you seldom cry normally but now you seem to cry all the time, this could be a symptom of depression. Increased sensitivity to other people's remarks or treatment of you can be a signal of depression. You feel hurt, rejected, abandoned, ignored, irritated, or unloved by

those close to you, and you want to withdraw from them. You think you may be overgeneralizing and overreacting to circumstances around you. Negative thought patterns seem to be more frequent and magnified.

4. *Loss of self-confidence.* You feel less capable. Trying new things is out of the question. You seem to lack initiative and self-motivation. What you once enjoyed doing now seems less meaningful. Your optimism is gone and life seems somewhat meaningless.

If you have a combination of some of these symptoms, you are probably suffering from depression. But there is hope. You are not alone. Even David the psalmist suffered depression. In Psalm 42:5 David asked, "Why are you downcast, O my soul? Why so disturbed within me? Put your hope in God, for I will yet praise him, my Savior and my God" (NIV). Psalms 42 and 43 are wonderful words to those in depression.

Here are some other specific helps.

1. *You are of tremendous value to God.* Your performance or feelings have no bearing on God's unchanging, unconditional love for you. He loved you while you were yet a sinner. He loves you now. His love (unlike that of some moms, dads, husbands, kids, and friends) is not based on performance. In Matthew 10:29-31 God tells us, "Are not two sparrows sold for a penny? Yet not one of them will fall to the ground apart from the will of your Father. And even the very hairs of your head are all numbered. So don't be afraid; you are worth more than many sparrows" (NIV).

2. *This too shall pass.* Even extreme depression can be overcome and cured. While you will need to find a way to uncover your emotions and get to the root of your depression, recognize that you will not always feel this way. *There is hope.* There is life after depression. Hang onto the principles and values of your past. Keep your roots in God and His Word even though it may give little comfort now. Stay as close as you can to your family and friends. Don't make drastic decisions or major changes now. Keep your value system intact.

3. *Seek help.* Depression is usually caused by covering up emotions. The longer we supress them, the more difficult it is for us to uncover them and rid ourselves of the cause of our depression. Unexpressed anger is sometimes a cause of depression. Seek out a professional *Christian* counselor to help you. A pastor can be a wonderful help and inspiration, but sometimes depression needs a professional form of therapy that a pastor may not be trained to give. Ask your pastor to refer you to a Christian professional who can give you all the help you need.

Depression can also sometimes be caused by physical problems, especially in women. It is a good idea to have a thorough physical checkup from your doctor. Certain cycles of life bring on severe chemical and hormonal changes in our bodies. These should not be ignored as a possible contributor to depression.

4. *Pray the Psalms.* The Psalms can be a wonderful help when we read them aloud as prayers to God. While this is not inevitably a cure for depression, it can be a wonderful source of comfort and encouragement as you identify with the psalmist and his sensitivity to human emotion.

RESOURCES

How to Deal with Depression. Timothy Foster. Victor Books, 1984. (An outstanding book on the subject of depression.)

Breaking Through: How to Overcome Housewives' Depression. Marie Morgan. Winston Press, 1983.

Changepoints. Joyce Landorf. Fleming H. Revell, 1981.

A Woman's Quest for Serenity. Gigi Tchividjian. Fleming H. Revell, 1982.

QUESTION 13

I don't feel good about myself. What can I do to feel better about me?

All of us start out as sweet, innocent little babies. And almost all babies (even those that are fat, bald, or have big ears) are thought to be cute, darling, beautiful, cuddly, etc. We love to adore them, pick them up, hug them, kiss them, humor them, and coo over them.

But somewhere along the line things begin to change. We "babies" are no longer the center of attention, and flaws begin to emerge.

Some of us are more fortunate than others. Some of us, in our childhood, have had someone (mother, father, other loved one) who loved us, believed in us, always expected the best from us, and was quick to see the good in us. That person made us feel so special that no matter what flaws others saw in us, we heard our loved one's voice and felt his or her encouragement and belief in us. Even so, some of the criticism for who and what we were still seeped through the protective shield of love.

Others of us were less fortunate. There were too many voices telling us we were inadequate and inferior. We were told of our failures...repeatedly. We began to see ourselves as ugly, or stupid, or clumsy, or unworthy. And we began to believe the charges.

It is these feelings that create self-hate, discouragement, and defeat in our lives. It's time now to open our eyes and see that all of us have flaws. Nobody's perfect. But remember too that all of us have value to God and have incredible

74

potential. A lot of the feelings you have about yourself were put there by someone else—people who felt inferior to you, or in their own hurt desired to hurt you too. Now let's consider the source and go back to God's smile of approval. He wants us to be free, fulfilled, and joyful. He wants us to appreciate His handiwork in creating us.

Here are some things to consider in discovering the real you—the you that God sees!

1. *God knew you before you were born.* Psalm 139 is designed for our misplaced generation. Here's what David said.

> O Lord, You have searched me and known me. You know my sitting down and my rising up; You understand my thought afar off. You comprehend my path and my lying down, and are acquainted with all my ways. For there is not a word on my tongue, but behold, O Lord, You know it altogether. You have hedged me behind and before, and laid Your hand upon me. Such knowledge is too wonderful for me; it is high, I cannot attain it.
>
> Where can I go from Your Spirit? Or where can I flee from Your presence? If I ascend into heaven, You are there; if I make my bed in hell, behold, You are there. If I take the wings of the morning and dwell in the uttermost parts of the sea, even there Your hand shall lead me, and Your right hand shall hold me. If I say, "Surely the darkness shall fall on me," even the night shall be light about me; indeed, the darkness shall not hide from You; but the night shines as the day; the darkness and the light are both alike to You.
>
> For You have formed my inward parts; You have covered me in my mother's womb. I will praise You, for I am fearfully and wonderfully made; marvelous are Your works, and that my soul knows very well. My frame was not hidden from You when I was made in secret, and skillfully wrought in the lowest parts of the earth. Your eyes saw my substance, yet being unformed. And in Your book they all were written, the days

fashioned for me, when as yet there were none of them.
How precious also are Your thoughts to me, O God!
How great is the sum of them! If I should count them,
they would be more in number than the sand; when
I awake, I am still with You (Psalm 139:1-18 NKJV).

Isn't that beautiful? God had your life planned. You are
not an accident. God began to shape and mold you before
you were born. There is a path to happiness and joy for you.
There is a plan of fulfillment that will bring satisfaction to
your life. I don't know what it is, but it is there for *you* to
discover.

2. *God wants to develop our potential.* There is nothing that
brings greater joy to the heart of God than to see us develop
and succeed in the plan and direction He has laid out for
us. In Ephesians 2:10 we are told that "we are His workman-
ship, created in Christ Jesus for good works, which God
prepared beforehand that we should walk in them" (NKJV).
Further, He tells us that when He begins this good work
in us, it is His plan and will to finish the work of blessing
us and filling our lives with His joy and peace.

3. *However, there are some basic reasons we do not like
ourselves, and we need to recognize these reasons and overcome
them.*

First, we listen to voices of criticism. Often we internalize
what we have been told. If you continually tell a child he
is "bad" or "stupid" or "lazy" or "ugly," before long he
or she will begin to believe these things are true. After all,
others see us as we really are. . . or do they? Often people's
remarks are born out of their own frustration or inferior feelings about themselves. It is a carnal, natural, human tendency to point out other people's flaws and put people down
or make fun of them.

One "you-have-big-ears" comment from some fourth-
grade peer, and we tend to want to hide our ears for the
rest of our lives. A teacher that conveys to us that we
are not as bright as others in the class, and we decide to
settle for academic mediocrity or failure for the rest of our

education, believing we are "average" or "stupid." Isn't that ridiculous?

True, not all of us are intellectual geniuses, Olympic athletes, or concert musicians, but we all have areas of excellence.

We need to start dwelling on the positive qualities that we possess rather than the flaws. After all, flaws may not really be flaws, but simply character that rounds out and puts emphasis on our qualities.

Second, some of us have suffered failure and we fear failing again. Someone has said, "He who aims at nothing will hit it every time." Fear of failure will eat away at us like a cancer. It will paralyze us into inaction.

It's an old saying, but true, that it is better to try and fail than not to try at all. *Don't give up!* Attempt again. You have ability, you have potential, you have God and all His angels cheering you on. *Go for it!* Reach a little higher, pick up the pieces, and move on with God in His strength and power. Ben Patterson says that happiness is "something to do, someone to love, and something to hope for." *You* have something God wants you to do and someone God wants you to love, and you have God's eternal plan for you to hope for!

Third, we listen to the wrong voice. Satan is said to be the accuser of the brethren. He is the one who will bring to remembrance all the past, all the wrong and destructive voices, and all the condemnation, guilt, accusations, and feelings of failure. He wants to defeat you, break you down, destroy you. And if you listen to him, *you will hate yourself.*

Start listening to God. Hear Him as He says to you, "God sent not his Son into the world to condemn the world, but that the world through him might be saved" (John 3:17). Hear Jesus as He says, "Peace I leave with you, my peace I give unto you; not as the world gives, give I unto you" (John 14:27) and "These things have I spoken unto you that my joy might remain in you, and that your joy might be full" (John 15:11).

God has every intention of seeing you full of peace, joy,

and fulfillment. He loves the you He has created and is developing. Start listening to His evaluation of you...I guarantee you'll like it!

4. *Learn that there is a distinct difference between outward beauty and inward happiness.* The world's image of beauty changes from age to age and culture to culture. With Eskimos, fat women are beautiful because of the necessity of keeping warm in a cold climate. In Africa, women adorn themselves with scars, tattoos, red mud smeared in their hair, and even pieces of wood imbedded in their lips to make them protrude out like a duck's bill. In America we have bony, half-starved women because "skinny" is in.

These are all outward appearances that have little to do with inner qualities or true happiness. So it is with other characteristics that we can't change, such as our height and the shape of our jaw, nose, mouth, ears, etc.

What we need to develop is our *inward qualities.* While we humans look on outward appearances, God looks on the heart. His standard of beauty is development of character and more of the fruit of the Holy Spirit (love, joy, peace, longsuffering, gentleness, goodness, faith, meekness, and self-control). It's more of the character and nature of Jesus Christ and less of the character and nature of the old me that translates into real beauty and happiness. And that's what attracts other people and draws me to love, appreciate, and accept myself.

5. *Learn that development of God's character within is more important than the world's standard of success.* We tend to measure success by the "stuff" of life—bank accounts, cars, houses, popularity, power, education, etc. But that is the *world's* standard of success. In the sight of God the Father, Jesus was the most successful of all men, and yet while on earth He had none of the things mentioned above. No "stuff." God was pleased when King Solomon, after being told by God that he could ask for and receive anything he wanted, asked for wisdom. This was an internal quality of character and not "stuff." It was Jesus who said, "Seek first

the kingdom of God and his righteousness, and all these things shall be added unto you" (Matthew 6:33).

Here are some positive steps you can take toward better self-acceptance.

1. *Thank God for who you are.* Some things you have no control over. Certain circumstances and parts of your life are beyond your ability to change or alter. These are the things that you must accept. The Bible tells us, *"In everything give thanks, for this is the will of God concerning you."* How glad I am that Scripture does not say, *"For everything give thanks"!* One cannot be thankful *for* personal failure, or *for* disease, or *for* circumstances that are unpleasant. But we can be thankful *in* any situation. This means that we learn to experience God's joy and peace regardless of our circumstances, recognizing that He knows our address and knows how we feel. Begin to give God thanks for all you are. Demonstrate thankfulness *in* all situations and you'll find your attitude about yourself and your circumstances begin to change.

2. *Put yourself back into God's hands.* God is never finished with us. This life is a continual school, and the wonderful thing about it is that no matter how many times we fail, no matter how many flaws we think we have, no matter how disadvantaged we have been in our childhood or past, to God we are all gems, precious in his sight. We need to let Him continue to mold, shape, and polish us. Romans 9:20,21 tells us, "But indeed, O man, who are you to reply against God? Will the thing formed say to him that formed it, 'Why have you made me like this?' Does not the potter have power over the clay, from the same lump to make one vessel for honor, and another for dishonor?"

Recognize that no matter what your condition, only the Master Potter has the power and ability to develop the inner beauty and character in you. His way is best, so you might as well put your life back into His hands.

3. *Learn the joy of serving others.* In other words, stop reflecting on your own faults, inadequacies, and disadvantages.

Start reaching out to other people. A cup of cold water in Christ's name will do much more for you than a pity party. Learn to be an *encourager* rather than a discourager. When you learn the gift of encouragement to others, something wonderful happens. Your encouragement to others becomes an encouragement to *you.* Your smile to others smiles back at you. Your bringing joy to another produces joy within you.

Stop dwelling on your own problems and start being a positive encouragement in other people's lives. You will be amazed at how completely this will change your image of yourself!

RESOURCES

Can You Love Yourself? Jo Berry. Regal Books, 1978.

What Wives Wish Their Husbands Knew About Women. James Dobson. Tyndale, 1975.

Woman's Search for Self-Esteem. Peter Blitchington. Thomas Nelson Publishers, 1982.

Part IV _____

Health

QUESTION 14

I'm overweight and have tried many diets, but nothing seems to work. Is there any hope for me?

We live in a society today that puts a tremendous premium on being *thin.* In many ways this has become a social obsession. Along with this obsession has come a virtual epidemic of eating disorders. Two of these are anorexia nervosa and bulimia. Anorexia nervosa is a disease (almost always found in women) that affects a woman's perception of herself. Even after she is thin or severely underweight, her mind tells her she is fat. Women with anorexia nervosa can literally starve themselves to death.

Bulimia is a disorder in which the victim will gorge herself on huge amounts of food (an eating binge) and then induce vomiting or take laxatives in order to rid her body of the food. The National Organization of Anorexia Nervosa and Associated Diseases estimates that there are more than one million sufferers of such diseases in the United States alone. Women constitute more than 90 percent of the cases to date.

Not quite as bizarre is the more common problem of being overweight. It is estimated that more than 50 percent of the American population is overweight.

Much of the problem with what we will call the American Eating Disorder can be traced to attitudes we hold about ourselves, along with emotional problems directly related to personal feelings about life, circumstances, and perceived self-worth.

In these pages we are not going to suggest another diet. There are thousands of nutritious diets in print today, and most of them will work if you stick to them. Rather, we want to deal with some of the underlying causes of eating disorders in an effort to help you get to the bottom of your problem.

Unlike alcohol, drugs, or a variety of other indulgences, food is a necessary part of human survival. We face it three times a day. Total abstinence or complete withdrawal is impossible. As a result, food is a reality that we must learn to control if we are ever to have healthy bodies and feel good about ourselves. We cannot escape eating!

Unfortunately for many of us, food is used to placate our emotional and subconscious needs rather than to simply nourish our bodies. Food can become the friend we don't have, the gratification we don't receive, or the reward we think we deserve but is not coming from those around us. Sweets especially act as a "treat" or "reward." Many of you can remember your parents telling you, "Eat your vegetables and you can have some chocolate cake." Or you have pleasant memories of stopping at the ice cream shop with your father, or getting candy in abundance at Christmas or Easter.

Throughout many of our lives, food has been used as a reward for good behavior. Now as an adult, these foods when ingested give us a good feeling about ourselves.

Often this good feeling induced by food is a compensation for negative feelings. Let's look at some of these.

1. *Low self-esteem.* When we don't feel good about who we are, or we think we are undesirable, ugly, or unlovable, we find temporary gratification by eating. We adopt it as a form of loving ourselves. It's a way of saying "You're okay, you deserve a reward." The problem is that the more we eat, the heftier we become! Next time we look in the mirror or shop for clothes, our self-esteem takes an even worse nose dive!

2. *Guilt.* Picture in your mind an emotional scale shaped like an old-fashioned balance scale. When more weight is put on one side, the scale tips in that direction. Placing additional weights on the other side will bring the scale in

balance. Guilt (either real or imagined) will tip our scale in one direction. Something inside us desperately wants the scale to stay evenly balanced. This means that we either have to rid ourselves of the guilt (via confession, restitution, etc.) or we have to stack something on the other side to balance the scale.

Food is often used to balance our guilt. Guilt is frequently accompanied by blame. We blame other people, God, or ourselves for the problem, offense, or circumstance. This often leads to a "pity party," and a pity party leads to a balancing compensation of *food,* the more calories the better to anesthetize the pain. This becomes a vicious cycle!

3. *Anxiety, stress, or worry.* Food in this case becomes our baby bottle, our security blanket. Tense feelings are subconsciously soothed by food. Experts agree that a much better solution to anxiety or stress is exercise. However, the easy thing to do is to eat those foods that have made us feel good before.

4. *Depression, laziness, and boredom.* Sugar is addictive. Varying levels of blood sugar can produce various moods and behavior patterns. Foods are frequently used subconsciously as a "drug" to change our feelings. Are you the kind of person who, when alone or bored, is tempted to head for the refrigerator or pantry? It's almost like saying, "I'm bored—let's have a party!"

Do any of these emotions ever fit your eating habits? Take a piece of paper and jot down the emotions you often struggle with. Here are some suggestions to help you with the battle warring inside you.

Beware of emotional needs that drive you to eat. If we Americans ate food only to placate our natural hunger (rather than as a social activity or to feed our emotional needs), most of our eating-disorder problems would drop drastically. Recognize the times when you are being an emotional eater, and find alternative ways to deal with your emotions. Write in your diary, read a book, get involved in a stimulating conversation, make love with your spouse, go shopping, or take a walk. The most important thing during times of emotional stress is to *avoid the kitchen.* Don't relieve your boredom, guilt, or low self-esteem by making a double batch of chocolate chip cookies!

Eat nutritious foods. Avoid junk foods, especially between meals. If you must eat between meals, keep some fruit, carrot sticks, celery, or other forms of low-calorie finger foods handy.

These may not "satisfy" like a piece of apple pie or a candy bar, but they will form a substitute that makes it easier to maintain self-control.

Consumption of certain nutritious foods is on the decline in America while consumption of junk food is on the increase. *U.S. News and World Report,* December 8, 1980, reported the following fattening foods on the incline.

Food	Consumed 1979 (per person)	% change since 1960
Soft drinks	37.5 gallons	Up 175.7%
Fats, oils, butter, margarine	61.2 lbs.	Up 26.2%
Sugar/sweeteners	137.0 lbs.	Up 26.2%
Refined flour, cereal products	150.0 lbs.	Up 2.0%

The same report showed the following nutritious foods on the decline.

Food	Consumed 1979 (per person)	% change since 1960
Fresh vegetables	144.3 lbs.	Down 1.2%
Fresh fruit	81.3 lbs.	Down 9.7%
Milk, cream	32.9 gallons	Down 12.4%
Eggs	274	Down 15.4%

Retrain yourself and your family to think *nutrition.*

Increase your level of exercise. Nothing will make you feel better about yourself than a good exercise program. Walking, jogging, swimming, tennis, or a host of other activities will make you feel better both physically and emotionally. Start slowly, but start now. You will be amazed at how much this will do for the real you.

Stop having a pity party over your weight problem. You are a multitalented, valuable person just the way you are. If you don't lose one ounce of fat, or even if you gain more, it will never diminish God's love for you.

Rise above the superficial society we live in and realize that real beauty goes far deeper than the shape and size of your legs. Begin to reach out to other people around you. Get involved with their lives. Examine the talents that God has given you.

If you want to lose weight, do it. But don't wait till you're down to 105 pounds to embark on the other talents and gifts that you have to offer. Start living a full life today.

RESOURCES

Image of Loveliness. Joanne Wallace. Fleming H. Revell, 1978.
Confessions of a Closet Eater. Jackie Barrile. Martin Press, 1983.

QUESTION 15

> ## I'm afraid I'll get cancer. How can I overcome this fear?

Good news: Everyone does not get cancer. Two out of three Americans will never get it.

Better news: Every year more and more people with cancer are cured.

Better-yet news: You can do something to help protect yourself from cancer.

Best news: God has everything in control of your life, and you can trust Him with your future!

The following facts about cancer have been published for public use by the National Cancer Institute.

In the past few years, scientists have identified many causes of cancer. Today it is known that about 80 percent of cancer cases are tied to the way people live their lives. For example, the food they eat, the work they do, and whether they smoke all affect their likelihood of getting cancer.

Once you know some of the factors that increase the possibility that you might get cancer, you can take some control over them. Some are hard to control (such as your work environment), but others are easy (such as eating good foods).

No one knows for sure how a normal cell becomes a cancer cell. But scientists agree that people get cancer mainly through repeated or long-term contact with one or more cancer-causing agents called *carcinogens*.

Scientists now believe that most cancers are caused in two

steps by two kinds of agents: *initiators* and *promoters*. Initiators start the damage to a cell that can lead to cancer. For example, cigarette smoking, X-rays, and certain chemicals have been shown to be initiators.

Promoters usually do not cause cancer by themselves. They change cells already damaged by an initiator from normal to cancer cells. For example, studies show that alcohol promotes the development of cancers in the mouth, throat, and possibly the liver when combined with an initiator, such as tobacco.

An agent that has been linked to the cause of a particular kind of cancer is called a risk factor. Contact with that agent increases an individual's likelihood (or risk) of getting that kind of cancer. Exposure to a particular risk factor does not necessarily mean that you will get the disease, but it does mean that the possibility that you might get cancer has increased. Risk factors are described in several ways.

There are "avoidable" and "unavoidable" risk factors. You can cut down or cut out your contact with avoidable risk factors, such as tobacco or alcohol. Unavoidable risk factors are those which you personally cannot control. For example, the risk of getting any type of cancer increases as you get older.

There are both "known" and "suspected" risk factors. A known risk factor is an agent that has been shown by either studies of human populations or by laboratory tests to be capable of producing cancer. A "suspected" risk factor is thought to produce cancer, although studies have not yet confirmed the link to cancer.

Of all the chronic diseases, cancer is the most curable. Today nearly half of all cancer patients can be cured by modern treatment methods. Great advances have been made in our ability to prevent, detect, and treat cancer.

Studies suggest that certain foods and some nutrients contained in those foods may be associated with the development of cancer.

Some findings suggest that a high intake of dietary fat is a risk factor for cancer.

Population studies indicate that obesity increases the risk of developing certain cancers.

Other studies suggest that some vitamins and dietary fiber may help protect you from developing some forms of cancer. Current evidence suggests that by choosing carefully and eating a well-balanced diet, you may reduce your cancer risk. For a well-balanced diet:

Eat a variety of foods every day. Include fresh fruits and vegetables, especially those high in vitamins A and C, such as oranges, grapefruit, nectarines, peaches, strawberries, cantaloupe, and honeydew melons. Choose leafy green and yellow-orange vegetables like spinach, kale, sweet potatoes, and carrots, as well as cabbage, cauliflower, broccoli, and brussels sprouts.

Keep your intake of all fats low, both saturated and unsaturated fats. Choose lean red meats, fish, and poultry. Trim fat from steaks, roasts, and chops, and skin poultry before cooking. Try broiling, roasting, or baking meats and fish, or simmering them in their own juices, rather than frying them. Limit your use of butter, margarine, cream, shortening, and vegetable oils. Avoid hidden fats in salad dressings and snack foods like potato chips. Choose low-fat or skim milk, low-fat cheeses, and dairy desserts. Choose fruit instead of high-fat desserts.

Eat food with fiber, such as whole-grain breads and cereals; a variety of raw fruits and vegetables, especially if eaten with the skin; beans, peas, and seeds. A well-balanced diet will help keep you from being either over- or underweight. You can lose weight by increasing your physical activity, eating smaller portions of food, and eating less sugar and sweets. Scientists have found some relationship between a lack of certain vitamins—A and C—and cancer. For example, diets low in vitamin A have been linked to cancers of the prostate gland, cervix, skin, bladder, and colon.

On the other hand, studies indicate that vitamins A and C may help protect the body from certain types of cancer. You can get all the vitamins A and C your body can use if you choose two helpings daily from the same fruits and vegetables that are in a balanced diet—dark green vegetables, yellow-orange vegetables, and yellow-orange fruits.[1]

People who smoke have a ten times greater chance of getting cancer than people who don't smoke. Overall, smoking causes 30 percent of all cancer deaths. The risk of getting lung cancer from cigarettes increases with the number you smoke, how long you have been smoking, and how deeply you inhale. Smoking also has been linked to cancers of the larynx, esophagus, pancreas, bladder, kidney, and mouth.

Repeated exposure to sunlight over a long period of time has been linked to skin cancer. The sun's ultraviolet rays harm the skin. These rays are strongest from 11 A.M. to 2 P.M. during the summer, so that is when risk is greatest. Fair-skinned people are at greater risk than dark-skinned people. They have less of a pigment called melanin in their skin to block some of the sun's damaging rays. The harm done is never fully repaired, even though the suntan or burn fades away. You can protect yourself from the sun's rays and still spend a lot of time outdoors. Wear a broad-brimmed hat. Use sunscreens. A number 15 on the label means that most of the sun's ultraviolet rays will be blocked out.

Use of the hormone estrogen has been linked to cancer of the uterus. Studies show that women who took large doses of estrogens for menopause symptoms have a greater risk of developing uterine cancer than women who did not take estrogens. Increases in risks to other cancers have been studied, but the results have been unclear. Birth control pills generally have not been linked to increased cancer risks and may lower the risk of ovarian cancer. Today, estrogens for menopause symptoms and for birth control can be prescribed at very low levels and with another hormone, progesterone, added. These two factors have reduced cancer risks greatly. If you are taking estrogens, you can help protect yourself by discussing dose levels and hormone combinations with your doctor.

The cause of breast cancer is unknown. There is a common misconception that an injury to the breast can cause breast cancer, but there is no evidence to support this. The injury usually calls a woman's attention to a tumor that is already there. About 95 percent of breast cancers are discovered by women themselves, often through the practice of BSE (breast self-examination).

Every woman should take the time to examine her breasts for signs of cancer. Once a month is often enough, and the best time is right after her period. After the menopause, any set day, such as the first of the month, is a good time to do BSE. Here is how to examine your breasts.

1. *In the shower.* Examine your breasts during bath or shower; hands glide easier over wet skin. Fingers flat, move gently over every part of each breast. Use right hand to examine left breast, left hand for right breast. Check for any lump, hard knot, or thickening.

2. *Before a mirror.* Inspect your breasts with arms at your sides. Next, raise your arms high overhead. Look for any changes in contour of each breast, a swelling, dimpling of skin, or changes in the nipple. Then rest palms on hips and press down firmly to flex your chest muscles. Left and right breast will not exactly match—few women's breasts do. Regular inspection shows what is normal for you and will give you confidence in your examination.

3. *Lying down.* To examine your right breast, put a pillow or folded towel under your right shoulder. Place right hand behind your head—this distributes breast tissue more evenly on the chest. With left hand, fingers flat, press gently in small circular motions around an imaginary clock face. Begin at outermost top of your right breast for 12 o'clock, then move to 1 o'clock, and so on around the circle back to 12. A ridge of firm tissue in the lower curve of each breast is normal. Then move in an inch, toward the nipple, and keep circling to examine *every part of your breast*, including nipple. This requires at least three more circles. Now slowly repeat the procedure on your left breast with a pillow under your left

shoulder and your left hand behind your head. Notice how your breast structure feels.

Finally, squeeze the nipple of each breast gently between your thumb and index finger. Any discharge, clear or bloody, should be reported to your doctor immediately.

The real hope for the future is in earlier detection. Cancer specialists all over the world are improving diagnostic techniques, learning more about the nature of "early" or "minimal" cancer, and developing more effective combinations of treatments.

Breast cancer is the most common form of cancer for women over 35. While it is true that one of every eleven women will get breast cancer, consider the other ten who will not! And today, through early detection and other treatment, nearly 85 percent of the women who do get breast cancer survive.

In an article in *Virtue* magazine, Dr. VanderVeer says, "A woman must remember that the emotional trauma of a breast tumor is usually worse than the physical trauma. We live in a very breast-conscious culture; indeed, society's outlook is directed toward the young, the glamorous, the physically beautiful. We must keep in mind, however, that physical transformations occur almost daily in human life, resulting from accidents or amputations of limbs or breasts because of injury or illness.

"The apostle Paul wrote, 'We have this treasure in earthen vessels' (2 Corinthians 4:7). This treasure, God's spirit and love, establishes a true and lasting beauty within us. Beauty as defined by today's standards often lasts only as long as the youth and perfection of the physical body. What a comfort to realize that even though our bodily vessels, like their biblical counterparts, can be scratched, cracked, and broken, the treasure of the Holy Spirit, God's true beauty, can never be taken from us."[2]

Fear is crippling and debilitating. God is not the author of fear, but Satan, the "father of lies," would have you live in dread of cancer. Fear keeps you from living the joyful, love-filled life that God intends His children to have.

After you are armed with facts on how best to take care of God's temple, your body, then you can be a good steward. That is your responsibility. Realize that ultimately we are God's responsibility. We can trust Him!

"For God has not given us the spirit of fear, but of power and of love and of a sound mind" (2 Timothy 1:7).

RESOURCES

Living Without Fear. Wilma Burton. Good News Publishers, 1981.

NOTES

1. Information taken from the brochure "Cancer Prevention" published by the National Cancer Institute, U.S. Dept. of Health and Human Services and the brochure "Facts on Breast Cancer" published by the American Cancer Society.
2. Dr. VanderVeer. "Beat the Odds," in *Virtue*, Sept./Oct. 1981.

QUESTION 16

> **I've been having a lot of tension and discomfort with my menstrual cycle. Could I have premenstrual syndrome?**

When I was a teenager I heard menstruation described as "the womb weeping for its loss." I thought it was a wildly poetic description. Now, years later, I'm not so sure it's poetic—but I have come to appreciate the complex way we are created. There's a lot of talk these days about "getting in touch with your feelings." Women who are experiencing difficulty with menstruation need to "get in touch with their cycles." Thankfully, new information on menstrual problems is now available.

Many women have real discomfort and mood swings (and generally feel out of commission) just before their menstrual flow begins. They could be suffering from Premenstrual Syndrome.

Symptoms of Premenstrual Syndrome

Psychological: irritability, lethargy, depression, anxiety, sleep disorders, crying spells, hostility.

Neurological: headaches (migraines usually occur the week preceding menstruation), dizziness, fainting, or (rarely) seizures.

Breasts: tenderness and swelling.

Gastrointestinal: constipation, abdominal bloating, abdominal cramping, craving for sweets.

Urinary: less frequent urination.

Skin: acne.

The most common psychological symptom of premenstrual

syndrome is tension. (In fact, many women refer to the whole syndrome as premenstrual tension.) There are three aspects to the tension: depression, irritability, and lethargy. The latest research shows that there actually is a physical cause for these symptoms.

One of the first physicians to become interested in PMS was Dr. Katrina Dalton, who practices in London. Dalton's theory is that PMS occurs as a result of the drop in progesterone levels that occur at the time of menstruation.

Other investigators have been studying prolactin, a hormone secreted by the pituitary gland in the brain. Prolactin controls the nursing reflex, and also has a role in controlling the output of ovarian hormones. It is known to be associated with water retention.

Dr. Penny Budoff also has done research with some very helpful results. In her book *No More Menstrual Cramps and Other Good News* she says:

> It seems to me likely that the solution to PMS has not been found because we have been looking for a simple solution to a complex problem. There probably is no single hormone or chemical that is responsible for premenstrual syndrome, but I have long felt that prostaglandins are involved.

Prostaglandins are found in nearly every cell of the body. They are derived from the essential unsaturated fatty acids in the diet and are broken down through a series of reactions to form prostaglandins. Prostaglandins are different from hormones in that they usually act where they are produced. (Hormones are produced in one organ—such as the pituitary—and go through the bloodstream to affect a distant organ, such as the thyroid.) Dr. Budoff goes on to explain:

> Prostaglandins regulate the tone of smooth muscles, the nonvoluntary muscles of the body. We cannot voluntarily control these muscles—the muscles of the blood vessels, the uterus, and the intestines, for

example—as we can control the muscles in our arms and legs that we command to contract to help us walk and work. Smooth muscles cause uterine contractions, change blood vessel diameter, and regulate intestinal activity—all without our conscious control. Smooth muscles are controlled, to some extent, by prostaglandin activity; and fluctuations in prostaglandin levels and ratios cause the muscles to react in different ways.... When prostaglandins are produced in excess amounts, the uterus is overactive and contracts too much, causing cramps and pain.

Some of the excess prostaglandin escapes from the uterus and into the bloodstream, where it may affect other smooth muscles in the body before it is destroyed. The smooth muscle of the gut is stimulated and contracts too rapidly and propels food along too quickly, causing diarrhea. The smooth muscle in blood vessels may cause blood vessels to constrict and dilate. That's why some women feel cold and hot flashes. And some women will faint because a sudden dilation of the blood vessels causes a pooling of blood in their legs and feet, depriving the brain of blood and oxygen.

... women with premenstrual syndrome have many symptoms that can be directly related to excess prostaglandin production. For example, they complain about joint pain or tenderness when they are premenstrual. We already know that patients who have arthritis have increased amounts of prostaglandins in their joint fluid. Most premenstrual women have sensations of lower abdominal cramping for three to four days prior to the onset of their periods, and it has already been documented that prostaglandins cause uterine contractions. The headaches that many women suffer premenstrually have been shown in some cases to be brought on by prostaglandins. Bowel habit changes and general discomfort are also due to prostaglandins. We also know that breast tenderness is related to an increase in cystic fluid accumulation and higher prostaglandin production by these cysts.

Just to round things out. . . prolactin increases prostaglandin production—and so does another well-known culprit, caffeine.[1]

Armed with these facts, you can alleviate premenstrual syndrome symptoms by doing several things:

• Ask your doctor about medication that inhibits prostaglandins.

• Reduce salt in your diet to prevent water retention. Avoid foods high in sodium, such as canned soups, bacon, hot dogs, commercial salad dressings, gravies, salted popcorn, etc.

• Increase protein in your diet, concentrating more on fish and poultry.

• Cut back on sweets and on foods high in carbohydrates. A craving for sweets may be due to low blood sugar levels.

• Reduce caffeine! This may alleviate tender breasts and headaches. Avoid coffee, tea, cola, and chocolate. Some women find they can tolerate one cup of regular or two cups of decaffeinated coffee per day. Experiment to determine your own sensitivity.

• Get involved in physical exercise. If you are not on a good exercise program, get on one! Take up walking, aerobic exercise, or jogging (of course with the recommendation of your physician).

Some women find it helpful to take these (available at your local drugstore). Check with your doctor:

Evening primrose oil—500 milligrams to 2 grams daily for two weeks prior to menstrual flow. If this doesn't help, then take it all month long.

Vitamin B-6—200-800 milligrams daily for two weeks prior to menstrual flow. Much higher doses may result in permanent nerve damage.

Vitamin E—600 units daily during the symptomatic period.

Magnesium—300-600 milligrams daily during the symptomatic period.

Calcium.

RESOURCES

No More Menstrual Cramps and Other Good News. Penny W. Budoff, M.D. G.P. Putnam & Sons, 1980.

NOTES

1. *No More Menstrual Cramps and Other Good News.* Penny W. Budoff, M.D. G.P. Putnam & Sons, 1980.

QUESTION 17

Does menopause have to be difficult?

I suppose every woman secretly dreads menopause. It carries with it connotations of being *old*, which in our current society does not have the value that *young and sexy* has. Subconsciously these messages become a part of our thinking, so to admit that we are indeed going through the "change" is tantamount to admitting we are over the hill.

Nothing could be further from the truth! First of all, realize that the subtle messages you're picking up from the maze of advertising, TV, and movies in regard to older women just aren't true. Men don't have to fight the "older" image as women do. A man's gray hair, increased personal income, and prestige in the community only seem to make him more attractive and distinguished. Too often older women feel useless, a "has been," or a "fading beauty." We desperately try to keep that youthful image with creams, makeup, and different styles, sometimes with pathetic results. What we need is a fresh perspective, an appreciation of ourselves. "I'm not getting older—just better" is true!

1. *What is menopause?* Menopause is the cessation of menstrual periods because of ovarian failure. The ovaries stop producing eggs, and the woman enters the postreproductive life, the final stage of sexual development. Many women "die" mentally and emotionally with their ovaries. *There is no need for this!* Although your body is going through tremendous physical changes that you must adjust to, you have every reason to be excited at the

prospects of a new, richer, and more productive life.

The main reason for physical and emotional problems at this time in your life is that your body is adjusting to the dwindling supply of estrogen that is being produced by the ovaries. As your body adjusts to the changes taking place during menopause, it helps to be aware of what you are going through at this time and to be "good to yourself." Understand that what you are feeling is *temporary*, and the symptoms can be relieved.

2. *What are the symptoms?* The symptoms can start six months to one year after total cessation of menstrual periods and may include:

- Fatigue (even though you've slept all night)
- Depression, mild to severe
- Tendency to gain weight
- Vaginitis, irritation, and itching
- Headaches
- Heart palpitations
- Loss of sexual desire, vaginal dryness
- Anxiety, irritation
- Hot flashes, night sweats
- Osteoporosis (bone loss due to calcium deficiency)

Of all women experiencing menopause, 20 percent have no problems during menopause, 10 to 15 percent have severe symptoms, and 65 to 75 percent experience symptoms in varying degree.[1] Besides the physical stress that women in menopause have, there are often other factors that make it generally a rough time. She may have aging parents that take a good deal of her time and consideration. Her own husband may be going through a midlife evaluation. Her children may be in college, or married, making her a new "grandma." It helps to have a sensitive, educated husband who will lovingly understand what his wife is going through.

3. *What can be done for the symptoms?*

Estrogen replacement therapy. This is a very popular, effective, and controversial treatment. It is easy to understand that if your symptoms are caused by dropping estrogen levels in your body, then replacing that estrogen under wise supervision from your physician should alleviate the symptoms. Estrogen replacement therapy can restore energy, provide more elastic skin, improve sleep, help lift depression, and stop hot flashes. But the most important reason for estrogen is to prevent *osteoporosis*, or bone loss (thinning of the bones).

Estrogen can, however, cause cancer of the uterus in certain people with high-risk factors. Scientists think the higher the dose, the greater the risk. In very low doses there seems to be no increase in cases of uterine cancer. But doses that are too low do not protect against osteoporosis.[2] When you are on estrogen, use the smallest amount that will still do the job. Read all you can on the subject, and thoroughly discuss your apprehensions and questions with your physician. Some doctors believe estrogen therapy to be so useful that if a woman is worried about getting uterine cancer, it's almost worth having the uterus removed.

There is a new therapy being used now—estrogen given for 21 days, then progesterone for ten days. Progesterone causes you to shed your uterine lining every month, making estrogen buildup almost impossible.

Lifestyle. This has to do with proper food and exercise. I know you've heard it many times, but you *must* take care of God's temple—you! We often abuse our bodies and then wonder why we don't feel well. Even if you don't feel like it, discipline yourself to begin exercising. Brisk walking is good. Set a time to exercise, and *stick with it.* Make a pact to go with your husband or a friend so that you can encourage each other. Aerobic and stretching exercises are excellent. This keeps your bones in better condition, lowers your heart rate and blood pressure, and alleviates depression. Go at your own pace (don't try to keep up with the 20-year-olds in the class!), but be consistent. If you're feeling tired, rest. Your body is gearing down, and you must adjust to a different pace.

Eat good food—lots of fresh fruits and vegetables—and cut

down on fats and sugar. About 1500 calories a day should be sufficient. To increase calcium in your diet (to prevent bone loss), include milk or milk products. Broccoli, clams, oysters, callards, salmon, and spinach are also high in calcium.

Mental attitude. Be positive as you look to the future! How you view life makes all the difference. Life is truly a great teacher, and there is much that you can share from your life experience.

Consider taking up a new career, or become involved in new mental challenges. Get involved in a Bible study. It is Scriptural for the "older women to teach the younger women." I think some older women have abdicated this role, and there is incredible potential going to waste in our churches.

When we go through different phases in our lives, we are forced to reevaluate our lives and priorities. Make this time an "oasis" where you can do personal reflection . . . time to enjoy your husband as you never have before . . . time to explore new avenues of creativity . . . time to meditate on God's Word.

> This I recall to my mind, therefore I have hope. Through the Lord's mercies we are not consumed, because His compassions fail not. They are new every morning; great is your faithfulness (Lamentations 3:21-23 NKJV).

In each "new morning" of our lives, in each new development, in each new challenge, God is there with His faithful provision. *He* never changes—praise God! His joy gives us strength.

RESOURCES

Forty-Plus and Feeling Fabulous. Ruby MacDonald. Fleming H. Revell Publishers, 1982.

Changepoints. Joyce Landorf. Fleming H. Revell Publishers, 1981.

NOTES

1. *Forty-Plus and Feeling Fabulous.* Ruby MacDonald. Fleming H. Revell, 1982, p. 68.
2. *The Woman Doctor's Medical Guide for Women.* Barbara Edelstein, M.D. Wm. Morrow & Co., 1982.

Part V

Parent/Child Relationships

QUESTION 18

> ## My husband and I disagree on child discipline. What's the answer?

It's not uncommon for a couple with a stable and harmonious relationship to find new areas of disagreement when a child is introduced into their family. No two families are alike, and often we see sharp disagreements not only over family traditions, sex, and finances, but also in methods of child discipline.

After all, both of you were raised by two completely different sets of parents with totally different temperaments and ideas for discipline. No wonder you come into a marriage with set ideas about raising children! Child discipline is seldom discussed during courtship or even early years of marriage. At that point all the attention is being focused on the couple and their adjustments to each other. We may discuss how large a family we want, general ideas about raising them in a Christian home, etc., but little is discussed about methods of discipline.

The act of disagreement, if played out in front of your children, can itself be most harmful to your child. Even infants can sense emotions and discord between a husband and wife, and when they sense that the discord is because of them, it can create unhealthy anxieties in a child.

Certainly it is all right to disagree, but do it in a calm, rational, *private* setting so that the children are not involved in the disagreement. Otherwise the child not only quickly learns how to manipulate one parent against the other, but will feel guilt and anger about it and can develop a myriad

of wrong emotional responses to pressure and crises.
Here are some guidelines that we hope will help.

1. *Spend time discussing child discipline.* Don't use one
method on the part of the husband and another method on
the part of the wife. Borrow from each other's ideas; be willing to compromise, and come up with a plan. A good family discipline plan will include discipline, reward, consistency, and love. In other words, a good discipline program
will have 1) a negative consequence when the child
deliberately disobeys or breaks the rules; 2) a positive consequence when the child makes an effort to obey the rules;
3) a *consistent* positive/negative consequence that is always
the same; and 4) an atmosphere of love, so that the child,
even when disciplined, knows that he is loved very much
by his parents.

2. *Decide on a plan and stick to it.* Work out an agreeable
plan that both of you are willing to follow, using the above
guidelines, and then *stick to it.* If necessary you can rediscuss
the plan and agree to revise certain parts that are not working as you expected. In fact, as your children go through
different stages of development, your plan should change
to accommodate the development of the child.

You may decide to spank your child during his early years,
but occasional withholding of privileges may work better
as he develops. The point is to have two parents working
together and supporting each other, along with a set of rules
that the entire family is thoroughly familiar with. This will
create a positive sense of security in your child. He will know
exactly where the boundaries are and how far he can go.

It pays to be consistent. Consistency will save you much
grief as your child grows up. Consistency not only produces
a much easier process for you, but also creates self-discipline
in your child.

3. *Always act out of love.* Any form of discipline that you
take when you are angry at your child will not produce the
desired results. Wait until you are calm and rational before
disciplining your child. There is a distinct difference between

punishment and discipline. Punishment is striking out at your child when you are angry, hurt, or frustrated. Punishment builds resentment and a sense of injustice within the child. Discipline, on the other hand, is a consistent consequence for wrong behavior and is recognized by the child as both loving and corrective even though it is painful. Discipline will build security, self-discipline, and self-esteem within your child.

4. *Support your spouse.* We've already said that it is important to agree, but even when you feel that your spouse overreacted or handled a situation poorly, *never* criticize him or her in front of the kids. Wait to discuss it later. Solidarity between parents is essential to building a strong fortress in your home.

5. *Learn to say you are sorry.* Your children will only learn true repentance from you. If they see you display anger, say unkind words to your spouse, or in other ways make observable mistakes (and we all make them!) they will carefully watch how you handle your mistake. How you respond will be internalized into their value system and will affect how they respond.

Frequently we parents, because of the authority role we play, display an "I'm never wrong" attitude. We do this by never apologizing in front of our kids and using excuses for our behavior.

I maintain that the best thing you can do in front of your kids is to humble yourself and say you are sorry and ask their forgiveness when you are wrong. Why? First, you are becoming a model to your children that says it is right to repent and ask for forgiveness. Second, you will gain greater respect from your children because they will see that you not only *express* certain principles and ideals but that you *practice* them. (They know when you're wrong even when you make excuses.) Third, you will open channels of communication with your child because he will trust you to be fair, honest, and loving in your counsel and response.

6. *Know when to spank your child.* There is a lot of debate

about spanking today, and so we include these comments on the subject. We believe that it is right to spank a child under the following guidelines:

When deliberate disobedience is observed. If a child is confused or does not understand what you want, a spanking will not accomplish its desired effect. However, if a child has deliberately disobeyed you, spanking can be an effective method of discipline.

When you feel in control. If you are angry, frustrated, or out of control, your discipline becomes punishment and is often more severe than the misbehavior. This can result in child abuse. Be sure you are in control of your emotions and have clearly analyzed the circumstances before spanking your child.

Avoid spanking your child:

When you are angry, frustrated, or out-of-control.

When the child reaches an age at which this form of discipline is no longer effective and other methods of discipline produce better results.

When a child is sick, distraught, extremely emotional, excessively tired, or otherwise not in the proper frame of mind to receive the discipline correctly.

7. *Recognize that children are different.* Our five children all respond differently. The rules are the same, but the method of discipline varies from child to child. Two of our children are very sensitive. A verbal scolding produces the same remorsefulness on them as a spanking on the other three.

Learn to tailor your plan to fit each child's emotional makeup. After all, the desired result is normal, healthy, loving, self-motivated children who grow up to be responsible, loving parents. Whatever way you feel this can be most effectively accomplished should be your rule of thumb in child discipline.

8. *Pray with your kids.* Regular prayer for guidance and help for your child's specific concerns and needs, as well as prayers of repentance and restoration after discipline, are

all a part of an effective child discipline program. Teach your child that *their* Source is the same as *your* Source. In this way prayer can become a powerful tool in raising your children and teaching them the principles you want them to acquire.

RESOURCES

Dare to Discipline. James Dobson. Tyndale, 1970.
How to Really Love Your Child. D. Ross Campbell. Victor Books, 1977.

QUESTION 19

My child is struggling in school. How can I best help him?

This is a frustrating problem because it is hard to be objective about your own child. Suppose the message is filtering through to you that your little Johnny has some real problems at school. You knew his papers weren't so hot, but you didn't know it was this bad. Now, according to his teacher, he's way down at the bottom of his class. You feel ashamed, irritated at Johnny for being lazy, and worried about his future. Many children who are emotionally and socially deprived struggle with schoolwork. But your child hasn't been deprived. So what have you done wrong?

Here are some guidelines that we have developed out of our own experience that can be of help to you.

1. *Don't waste time blaming yourself!* Mothers are awfully good at guilt. When fathers are confronted with their children's weaknesses or problems, they seem to find it easier to be objective about the child or the school. When mothers are faced with their child's problem, it becomes *their* problem! Our children are gifts from God that have simply passed through us into the world. We are their caretakers and guardians, and we answer to God for their care.

But each child is unique. Parents often subtly compare their children, sometimes not even aware that they are doing this. If you must compare, compare strength with strength. Don't compare your child's weaknesses with another child's strength. Sitting around worrying or feeling guilty is wasting precious time and energy. Now is the time for you to take positive steps to help your child. If *you* don't lobby for your child, who will?

2. *Get involved with the school and find out where the problem lies.* Your child's teacher will genuinely appreciate your interest once he or she realizes that you are not there to confront or blame. Let the teacher know right away that you are concerned, that you want to help make his or her job easier. Listen to what your teacher has to say about your child. You may have a preconceived idea of what the problem is. Listen to the teacher with an open mind. Your school should have access to professional testing services to see where your child needs help. Ask for these if the situation warrants it. Then ask for a consultation with these professionals. As a parent, you have a right to see all of your child's testing results and records. If your child needs extra help at school, it is his right to receive that help. A teacher should never give up on a child. Unfortunately, teachers are human, and not perfect. If your teacher does not have any constructive suggestions, be persistent. If necessary, go to the principal or school counselor for help.

There are many children who have learning disabilities. Betty B. Osman, author of *Learning Disabilities, A Family Affair* (Random House, 1979), prefers to call it "learning differences." These are children who cannot learn as other children do. Learning problems cover a wide range of difficulties. Much is now being found out about it, and *help is available.* "A child is considered to have a learning disability (rather than to be intellectually impaired) if he has extreme difficulty in certain areas of learning that do not seem commensurate with his ability."[1]

Reading disabilities, often called *dyslexia*, make up the largest group of learning disabilities. Within reading disabilities there are several groups.

Dyseidetic—Children whose reading and spelling errors show an inability to identify groups of letters in patterns or visual details. Such children spell words by sound—

"laugh" might be "laf." These children read slowly because they must sound out each word instead of relying on a repertoire of visually recognized words.

Dysphonetic—Children who are unable to relate symbols to sounds and cannot develop *phonetic* word-analysis skills. Such children make bizarre spelling errors unrelated to the sound of the word ("rough" might be "refer"). The dysphonetic reader can identify words he has memorized but cannot use phonetics to sound out new words.

Mixed—Children with a mixed type of dyslexia. These present the most difficult problem.[2] Have your child tested professionally to see where the problem lies.

Children with learning difficulties can learn to live with their problems, but they need help in tutoring.

Perhaps your child is too young for his grade. Some children mature later than others, especially boys. According to Betty Osman, "To justify retaining a child in a grade higher than kindergarten or first grade, one should be able to predict that the child should be consistently performing at least in the middle—or better, at the top—of the class by next year. If, on the other hand, it seems he will still be on the bottom academically, question the advisability of such a move.... For retention to be successful, the *whole* child has to benefit from the additional year."[3]

It may be that your child is struggling simply because he has some behavior problems that can be corrected: laziness, preoccupation, worry. After discussing the problem with your child's teacher, be perceptive. Pray for wisdom. James 1:5 says, "If any of you lack wisdom, let him ask of God, who giveth liberally...." This verse means what it says! The Lord gives us wisdom in correcting and disciplining our children. An excellent book on teaching children responsibility is *Making Your Children Mind Without Losing Yours*, by Kevin Leman (Fleming H. Revell, 1983).

3. *Work out a mutually acceptable plan with your child's teacher to help your child.* Find out what motivates your child and use it to encourage his efforts at learning. Our junior

high son, an avid sports fan, was successfully motivated to get a certain grade point average in order to play sports. Our younger son was motivated by stickers on a chart for certain accomplishments. You know your child best. After conferring with the teacher as to what would be a desirable goal, decide on a plan to reach it. Start with attainable, short-term goals, then work up to longer-term ones.

4. *Make home a haven.* Your home is the "launching pad" for your child into the world. Give him a good start! If your child is struggling at school, he needs all the help he can get from you to succeed (*not* pity, but good practical help). He *can* overcome difficulties, he *can* feel successful. It's your job to make sure he has the basic requirements to face the world:

• *Regular, nutritious meals.* A wholesome breakfast is essential for a good start to the day.

• *Enough sleep.* Children who are chronically tired can't perform at their best. You know how you feel if you don't have enough sleep.

• *Pleasant environment.* Is his room pleasant? Does he have a specific place where he can keep his belongings? Is he learning how to take care of his room? Routine is good for children who are struggling with learning. If children become organized at home they will become organized at school. Get him a bulletin board of his own so he can keep track of things that he needs to do.

• *Regular prayer.* Sit on his bed at night and spend time talking and praying with him. This will help him to open up and realize that the Lord is concerned with any needs he might have and that all the resources of heaven are available to him. You can help foster a lifelong trust in God in this way. Read the Scriptures to your child in palatable doses, doing this at a consistent time so that it will become a habit with your child as he grows older.

• *The wonder of books.* Get some books that he has success with and have him read to you. Take an exciting book and read a chapter every evening. Read one page and have your child read the next. That way he stays interested. This simple exercise helps immensely. *Keep at it!* Your child may want you to do all the reading, but resist! The idea is to get *him* to read. Become a regular visitor to the library, and take your child with you. You may have to "sneak" learning in: Play word games and spelling games in the car. It will take some effort on your part to help your child learn, but *you can do it.* Ask the school for resource material to work on at home. School personnel are usually delighted to give you helpful material.

• *Restricted TV.* During the school year, the TV is never on during the week (except for news) at our house. This simple rule has helped more than any one factor with our children and their homework. One statistic reported that the average TV is on in American homes 6.5 hours per day. This may be one reason many of our children are reading poorly.

5. *Find your child's strong points and encourage them.* Each child has strengths and weaknesses. A learning difficulty is not the end of the world, nor does it signify that your child will not be a success. Albert Einstein, Winston Churchill, and Nelson Rockefeller, among many successful individuals, all had learning difficulties. Success breeds success, and you need to find your child's strength.

Don't make a big deal out of your child's learning problems. Let him know you're concerned, but only enough so that the two of you do something constructive to help. Arm yourself with facts, then tackle the problem matter-of-factly and encourage him instead of nagging him. Nagging is concentrating on the *problem.* Encouraging him is concentrating on the *solution.* We parents are our children's cheerleaders, and a child struggling to learn needs a bit more "cheering on" at certain times in his life.

RESOURCES

Helping Children with Learning Disabilities. Ruth D. Rowan. Abingdon, 1977.

You and Your Child's Problems. Grace Ketterman, M.D. Fleming H. Revell, 1983.

Learning Disabilities: A Family Affair. Betty B. Osman. Random House, 1979.

How to Improve Your Child's Education. John Dobbert. Harvest House Publishers, 1980.

For further information on Learning Disabilities, write to:

> The Society for Children & Adults with Learning Disabilities
> 4156 Library Road
> Pittsburgh, PA 14234
> (Enclose stamped, self-addressed envelope)

NOTES

1. *Learning Disabilities: A Family Affair.* Betty B. Osman. Random House, 1979.
2. *Children with Handicaps: A Medical Primer.* Mark L. Batshaw, M.D. and Yvonne M. Perret. Paul H. Brookes Publishing Co.
3. *Learning Disabilities: A Family Affair,* op. cit.

QUESTION 20

> ## One of us wants more children and the other doesn't. How can we resolve this?

Some people have decided well before marriage what they feel is the perfect size for a family. Usually their rationale is based on personal feelings. Maybe they grew up in a large family and have very fond memories, or maybe they were an only child and had unpleasant memories, opting to have more children. Some, on the other hand, grew up with negative feelings about being one of seven or eight kids and have decided emphatically not to have lots of kids.

Often when we begin our families there is agreement that we want children. When you both decided to start your family, you probably expressed your feelings with thoughts like "We're ready to start our family and we want to experience the joys of being a parent."

Included in this expectation were pregnancy, birth, fixing up the room, participating in the love and joy wrapped up in this new life, and watching your child grow and develop. In addition, you probably reasoned that having a child is the normal thing to do and the ultimate goal of becoming "one flesh" (after all, this precious new life is one-half of each of you). No doubt Grandma and Grandpa as well as other members of both your families were happy with the news.

Some couples who have had more than one child reasoned that the first child needed a brother or sister to play with. Often the rationale goes like this: "Now that we have a boy/girl we're going to try for a (whichever it is we didn't get the first time)."

Most people would probably not question this line of reasoning. After all, children are wonderful gifts from God to love and cherish.

For many couples, after two children a new dynamic sets in. While some couples still *plan* a large family, many couples who have a third child (a fairly common happening) just sort of let it happen. Maybe it's in trying one more time for the boy/girl they still don't have, or maybe it's sort of "unplanned" but not too unwelcome. Some couples begin to ask themselves more seriously (especially if it's the third child of the same sex), "Just how many kids *are* we going to have?"

The ideal family size can be determined only by the ups and downs of marriage and life's circumstances. Some couples will decide that the first child should be the last, while others are restricted biologically due to health or pregnancy problems.

No "number" is perfect, nor is any family size going to assure a marriage all the things wanted in life. Sometimes family size is restricted to assure the enjoyment for more freedom and more things. But this is not an instant formula for a perfect family. In fact, a wonderful solidarity often emerges in large families, a growing awareness of togetherness and love that does not occur in smaller families. On the other hand, some parents have been able to give more attention to children with unique talents or special needs in a smaller family.

The average size of the American family has steadily declined. In 1960 the average family size (including adults) was 3.67. In 1970 it dropped to 3.58 and in 1980 to 3.29. It is estimated that by 1990 the average size will be 3.0 (based on current trends). That will mean only one child per family. At some point this trend will have to reverse itself or else we will decline in strength as a nation.

Personally, we love large families. We have five children and are grateful to the Lord for each one. If both of you as husband and wife agree that you want a large family, and you have the emotional makeup and resources to handle it, we would counsel you to go ahead and enjoy as many children as you can handle and take care of.

However, this is an issue that requires agreement by you and your spouse before having any more children. The decision to have more children has to be considered in light of both parties' motives for wanting more (or not wanting more), along with the emotional stability of your marriage and each spouse, and what you prayerfully feel is God's will for your family.

This answer is written to the couple where *one* partner of the marriage has doubts about having more children.

At whatever stage in family size one spouse begins to question family size (no kids, one, two, three, or more), it is indeed an important concern to resolve. Here are several questions and considerations for the two of you to discuss.

1. *What are your goals in life?* Often when two married partners sit down and discuss their future, they come up with startlingly different ideas about how they would like to spend the rest of their lives. Do you want more freedom to travel or to pursue other interests? How do more children fit into your plans?

Beware of selfish motives, and remember that having less children to gratify ''wants'' is not an automatic key to happiness. You may regret this decision later in life. However, there are realistic concerns that need to be addressed.

2. *Where are you now in life?* How old are both of you? How old will you be when a new child would be 18 if the wife were to conceive now? Do you feel that both of you are in sufficiently good health to survive the rearing of this child to age 18?

3. *What is your financial picture?* Can you afford another child? Does it mean the wife would have to quit work (or go to work)? How will this alter your lifestyle? What about saving for your children's college tuition?

4. *Is your marriage solid?* If your marriage is ''rocky'' and you have some doubts as to whether you and your spouse

will eventually resolve the problem, bringing another child into the world will not solve your marriage problem and could become a broken-home disaster for the new child.

5. *What is your emotional makeup?* Do both of you feel you can handle another child? What kind of stress will this create? Remember that each new child adds a new interpersonal dynamic to your home. When there are just two people (husband and wife) there is only one interpersonal relationship (husband/wife). When one child is added, there are three interpersonal relationships (husband/wife, father/child, mother/child). When a second child is added there are *six* interpersonal relationships (husband/wife, father/child 1, mother/child 1, father/child 2, mother/child 2, child 1/child 2). Each subsequent child adds several interpersonal relationships, any or all of which can add stress and emotional tension to the entire family. If you have five children (like we do), you have *21* interpersonal relationships! Frequently there are more than one of these relationships that are under tension or emotional stress or are temporarily "out of sync." How well do you handle friction? How well do you handle sibling rivalry? At what age will you be when most of your children are teenagers, and how well will you handle this growing stage?

These may sound like negative or pessimistic questions, but ask any parent who has raised a large family in today's society, and you will quickly see that they are very important considerations.

6. *How organized are you?* Large families take an incredible amount of organization and cooperation. Are you and your spouse planners, or do you just sort of let things happen? How big is your home? Can it be expanded if necessary, or can you afford a bigger one? What about quality time with each child (school functions, Little League, piano lessons, church activities, fishing trips, one-on-one conversations, reading-together time, etc.)? What about your own projects (hobbies, job, recreational activities, church activities)? How will these affect or be affected by another child?

7. *How flexible are you?* People who have rigid ideas about organization and lifestyle have a much more difficult time with large families.

8. *Is it too soon or too late to have another child?* "Two under two" can be a disaster for some people but perfect for others. Will this child be alone a lot of his adolescent years because of much older siblings?

9. *Have you prayed about another child?* Bringing another life into the world is an awesome responsibility. It affects not only you but your spouse, your other children, and ultimately the new child. Ask God to give you guidance so that you feel His leading in the matter. This is the most important factor in your decision. Both of you should feel the peace and confirmation of God in your decision.

Here are some typical reasons that people give for having more children. In our opinion they are not sufficient by themselves to warrant having another child.

"I come from a large family and have always wanted a large family of my own." This does not necessarily mean that a large family is best for you. All the factors mentioned above must be taken into consideration. You may have very fond memories of your childhood in a large family, but this doesn't mean that history will repeat itself. By the same token, you may have come from a large family that was unpleasant, and now you feel that you want to restrict the size of your own family. Be careful not to repeat your own childhood in the lives of your children. They are unique, with different temperaments. You and your spouse are different. Find out what's best for you and your family.

"I still want to try to have a boy" (or vice versa if you have all boys). Beware of this motive. There are people who have six boys or eight girls and still no child of the opposite sex.

Remember that under normal sperm counts, the odds are still 50/50 for each child at the time of conception. Just because you've already had two or three of one sex, *this does not increase your odds that the next one will be of the opposite sex.* It's like a coin flip. Even though it came up "heads" five times in a row, the next flip of the coin is still a 50/50 probability. If you really want a child of the opposite sex, why not consider adoption?

"I feel I need another child." Most women experience a need or strong desire to have a child. If this emotional need reoccurs with you after you have experienced the joys of having children, but other factors indicate that your family is as large as it should be, it's possible that your emotional needs are not being met in other ways.

Beware of the emotional need to keep having children. Emotional needs translated onto a child can be harmful. Assess your relationship with your spouse and see if there are needs that are not being met. Visit with a qualified counselor to explore why you feel an emotional need to have more children.

We feel that it is wise to be cautious about having more children when one spouse is having doubts. There are several reasons for this.

1. The "blame factor" can destroy a marriage when one spouse is pressured into having more children but later regrets it and resents his or her spouse for the decision (and also subconsciously resents the child).

2. You need to carefully consider the quality of time that you as a parent have available to spend with each child in the fast-paced world we live in.

3. Any parent who genuinely does not want another child should not have one. The child's future is just too critical.

4. It is usually easier for the parent wanting more children to adjust to *less* than it is for the partner wanting less children to adjust to *more*.

Please note that this entire discussion is based on the assumption that you are *not* pregnant now. If you are already pregnant and contemplating an abortion, you will have to look elsewhere for an excuse to abort your child. We firmly believe that life begins at conception and that abortion is the taking of a human life. Responsible decisions on whether to have more children should always be decided *before* pregnancy occurs.

RESOURCES

Under the Apple Tree: Marrying, Birthing, Parenting. Helen Wessel. Bookmates International, 1981.

Family Planning the Natural Way: A New Approach. Josef Roetzer, M.D. Fleming H. Revell, 1981.

QUESTION 21

> **With the prevalence of homosexuality today, how can our children grow up to have healthy sexual attitudes?**

Some parents do suffer anxiety about their children becoming homosexuals. Twenty years ago homosexuality wasn't commonly discussed, but today homosexuality is on the rise. Our society has been bombarded by militant homosexuals and lesbians proclaiming their "freedom" and their "superior lifestyle."

God did not create three sexes! He created two, male and female, thus creating mankind (Genesis 2). Would it be compassionate of us to say to someone who has cancer, "You just have to accept that you have cancer," and not offer any medical help? Of course not! We would do all we could to help. Many cancer patients are being helped and cured today. Hating homosexuals isn't the solution. To many Christians, homosexuals are the lepers of our society, but God intends for us to have the confidence and security to offer solutions and help for people who have become sexually confused.

Realize that there is a spirit of perversion. Be discerning. One reason we are not in favor of the Equal Rights Amendment is because of the influence it will have if it passes. Although equal rights for women is desirable, this bill is being used by militant homosexuals to promote their cause. The National Gay Task Force is one of the original supporters of the ERA.

Children's sexual awareness these days is precocious! From TV, movies, and playground talk, sexual identity is learned and formed in childhood. Influence of the home and parents are the most powerful influence, however. It may be difficult to think of your child as a sexual person, but he or she is!

Shortly after we adopted Amy, then three, I heard my seven-year-old son say, "Just what I thought—dolls all over the house!" It's been fascinating to watch the *difference*. Our boys seemed to come with a built-in *vrooom*! They love competitive sports. Amy likes action too, but she doesn't have the aggressive, competitive drive that the boys have. She is fascinated with clothes, "pretty" things, and playing with her "babies." I watched Andy, her big brother, from the kitchen window as he parted some bushes very carefully for his little sister to walk through. The protective, tender look on his face was priceless!

The best way to give your child a healthy sexual identity and to combat the influence of the day is by your own example. You can do this by reinforcing your husband as the man of the house. Even if he is absent due to death or divorce, he is a tremendous influence on your children *by what you project or say about him.*

Sadly, some children and teenagers are experiencing sexual confusion today. Some of today's top male teenage idols are effeminate. Experts agree, however, that early detection of sexual confusion of children and teens can be cleared up by a discerning, caring parent.

From the latest findings and case histories of homosexuals, it is becoming increasingly evident that fathers have a tremendous amount of influence on sexual identity. With divorce on the increase, many fathers become distant or preoccupied with midlife crisis. Or they're simply gone. That leaves Mother in the home. If you're a single parent, don't panic. Reinforce the good points of your husband to your children. If you are personally bitter about him, don't put that burden on your children. It isn't their problem.

Be sensitive in what you say to your children about their

sexual identity. Often parents have anxieties that are needless.
Peter and Barbara Wyden in *Growing Up Straight* warn:

> . . . We feel compelled to caution every parent *never*
> to plunge into any direct action of any kind about such
> worries without careful thought and preparation. Pre-
> homosexual tendencies in young people almost never
> represent an immediate emergency . . . [it is] a complex
> tangle. There are many opportunities for parents to
> reverse a child's drift into homosexuality. Here it is
> essential only to establish one key fact: any weaken-
> ing of a child's sense of masculinity or femininity takes
> a long time to develop before it erupts into active
> homosexuality. It also takes a long time to counteract.
> Hopefully, such a tendency will be spotted so early by
> an informed parent that it becomes unnecessary to dis-
> cuss the problem with a young person in the threaten-
> ing terms of homosexuality specifically.
>
> It is of utmost importance that parents avail them-
> selves of opportunities to counteract homosexual
> tendencies without meeting the problem head-on be-
> cause personal, accusing talk of homosexuality with a
> child, or even an adolescent, unless guided by profes-
> sional advice and carefully geared to the individual
> situation, can heighten anxieties and cause further
> damage by increasing a youngster's existing doubt
> about masculinity or femininity. . . . [1]

Be alert to unhealthy family conditions. Recent research has
shown that fathers actually seem to have an *absolute veto
power* over the homosexual development of their sons. Even
in cases where the mother was the smothering, domineer-
ing type, if the father or stepfather took his rightful place,
he could "save" the child.

Dr. Irving Bieber did an intensive study of 106 homosexuals to find out what their parents were like. It seemed
that the child who became a homosexual was usually over-
protected and preferred by his mother. In other cases he
was underprotected and rejected. In a large percentage of
the cases, the mother:

- acted dominating
- acted overprotective
- made the son her favorite
- made the son excessively dependent
- tried to make an alliance with the favorite son against the husband
- "babied" the son
- was unduly concerned about protecting the son from physical injury
- actually behaved in a seductive way toward the son.

The quality of love that a father gives, or even the memory of it being reinforced by the mother, seems critical. Of the fathers in the study, most:

- spent little or no time with their sons
- had a "detached" attitude toward their sons when they did see them
- were feared by their sons
- were hated by their sons.

Only a small percentage actually respected their fathers. From the research available, it seems that physical affection and hugging from both parents is essential.

In the same study by Dr. Bieber, he found that mothers of lesbians tend to be excessively bossy, hypercritical, and harsh. Their daughters are often fearful of them. These mothers may go out of their way to undermine their daughter's femininity (not dressing them in feminine clothes), and can be cruelly critical of the girl's appearance. Many such mothers demand that the child make the mother the center of attention. The mother often tears down the husband verbally in front of the daughter. Fathers can be crude or autocratic, but more often tend to be passive, ineffectual, and easily bossed by their wives. Dr. Irving Bieber says, "Fathers who are openly affectionate and masculine with their daughters and are strong figures in the family do not produce lesbians."

Such incidents in themselves do not produce homosexuals. It is constant, consistent scenes that can produce this sexual confusion. Authorities agree that it is just about impossible for a homosexual to be raised in a sexually normal home. A sexually normal home would be one that is not sexually overstimulating (a lot of nudity, children witnessing sexual intercourse of parents) or the other extreme—parents morbidly fearful of sexual inclinations, demonstrating extreme suspicion and overreaction to such things as masturbation.

Watch for early symptoms of sexual confusion. Among boys, according to Dr. Bieber, watch for an "anxious-to-please, lovely child; overly-polite, charming to adults; doesn't care for sports; avoids physical fights; excessively afraid of physical injury; 'lone wolves'. . . ." These fears are traceable to the mother's overconcern.

Lesbianism is almost impossible to define in pre-adolescence. "Tomboy" characteristics are no grounds whatever unless accompanied by other symptoms, such as: A girl says she wants to be a boy; habitually refuses to play with dolls; is habitually frightened of normal contacts with boys; does not like girls' games'; does not like to "play house"; is generally more competitive than normal girls; has temper tantrums directed against her mother; develops intense crushes on other girls, a teacher, or some other beloved adult; doesn't like boys at ages 13 to 14; has a general disdain for men.

Be alert to peer pressure. Never allow children to call "names." If your child needs good friends, take the initiative and encourage healthy friendships. It will take effort on your part, but it's worth it. Invite the friends over for the day, or take them to a fun event.

Parents need to know the facts: *Homosexuality can be prevented.* People are not born homosexuals. God has created us male and female. To reject what God has made us is rebellion against our Creator. Our minds must be constantly renewed by His Word and Spirit so that we are not subtly undermined by our society. "I beseech you therefore, brethren, by the mercies of God, that you present your bodies a living sacrifice, holy, acceptable to God, which is your reasonable service. And do not be conformed to this world, but be transformed by the renewing of your mind, that you may prove what is that good and acceptable and perfect will of God" (Romans 12:1,2 NKJV).

RESOURCES

Growing Up Straight. Peter and Barbara Wyden. Stein & Day, 1968.

How to Teach Your Child About Sex. Grace H. Ketterman, M.D. Fleming H. Revell, 1981.

How to Teach Children the Wonder of Sex. Dr. and Mrs. J. C. Willke. Hayes Publishing Co., Inc.

NOTES

1. *Growing Up Straight.* Peter and Barbara Wyden. Stein & Day, 1968, p. 61.

QUESTION 22

> ## My children are constantly fighting. How can I get them to stop?

Nothing can drive parents up the wall faster than fighting kids. There are a lot of books you can read on the subject, but don't be surprised if, while you've got your head buried in a book, your kids start fighting with one another! You just have to accept the fact that *some* bickering "comes with the territory."

Brothers and sisters under the same roof are brutally honest with one another. Home is where they can be "real." No party faces here. In family structures children learn to appreciate the divergence in people.

Families with fewer children sometimes have more intense sibling rivalry than families with more children. It's possible for parents to become overly involved and preoccupied with their children, scrutinizing the nuances in every word they say. If you feel you are always in the middle, always solving arguments, always breaking up fights, you are probably too involved in the conflict. Your kids have succeeded in getting you right in the fray with them—just what they wanted. Regardless of how they get it, your kids want to be number one with you. Don't stoop to arguing with your children. Back off, get in control, and be the parent.

Be especially aware of conditions that spawn unrest. Here are some specific needs that children must have met.

1. *The need to feel number one with the parent.* Every child has a right to be "special," or to feel like an "only child" once in awhile with his parents. This can be conveyed in

small but effective ways. Kids have a keen sense of what's fair. A lot of wars have started in history because someone felt a great injustice had been done.

"Who do you like best, Mom—me or him?" This question strikes terror in the hearts of parents who want to be viewed as "fair." This doesn't mean you have to give each child an identical toy, identical clothes, etc. In fact, this heightens the problem. But each child can know that you realize he's special. You can show this in various ways.

A. *His own space.* Even if the child doesn't have his own room, he should have his own drawer, or shelf, or nightstand—something that is uniquely his own space. And then be sure that the other kids learn to respect his "space." There are a lot of things that our own children have in common— toys, sports equipment, etc.—but there are a few things that are definitely each child's *own.* If a child feels respected he won't have to fight and scratch for recognition.

B. *Tangible evidence.* Each of our children has a baby book that he or she delights in looking through. Besides that, they have school scrapbooks, awards, and places to keep stories and poems that they have written. Then there are numerous family albums. We keep these things in a cedar chest, and occasionally the kids like to get them out and pore over them. Even our teenagers love this. They can look back over their "history," seeing the things that we have kept and treasured. This helps build a sense of identity.

C. *Special days.* Birthday celebrations are great because they are the perfect opportunity to really make the child feel like a "star." In our house, the birthday child gets to pick the menu and the way he celebrates his special day. Other holidays are important too. Kids love celebrations. At Thanksgiving, add individual touches—such as a special Scripture on each placecard, chosen particularly for that child. Easter at our house is almost as big a celebration as Christmas. We have an Easter hunt (like a scavenger hunt), using notes and riddles to find the special Easter "surprise" for each child. We get our children gifts with a spiritual significance—a Bible, Christian book, or music. With the final surprise we always put out a big sign: "Hallelujah! He Is Risen!"

Each of these special days or celebrations is the perfect time to tell each child, in little individual ways, that he or she is special.

2. *The need for something interesting to do.* The old saying "Idle hands are the devil's workshop" is really true! I have often thought of our four energetic sons as four little "bulls" with energy just begging to be put to use. Not directing that energy is similar to revving motors up in supercharged cars, then turning them loose without drivers, hoping they won't have a collision. Each child has different talents and abilities. Parents need to discern what they are and encourage them. Sports, reading, writing stories, music lessons, band, art, making things—each child has an area that can be his specialty—something that says, "I am *me.*"

There are times, even with their varied interests, that kids get squirrelly and just bug each other. This is the time to redirect. Assign jobs (wash the car, stack the wood, do the dishes, make cookies, etc.). Pull out projects—painting, Play-Doh, or coloring, depending on the children's ages and abilities. *Redirect* that energy *away* from each other and *toward* other things. When things start heating up between your kids and *you* start heating up as a reaction (and you hear yourself saying a lot of things that begin with "Don't—" "Stop—" and "Quit—"), *redirect that energy to positive use.*

3. *The need for spiritual guidance.* My 13-year-old son Eric and I were riding down the road together, discussing why kids fight. I asked Eric, "Tell me honestly. Why do you think kids fight?" He thought a brief second and then said, "Selfishness. We just want our own way." I immediately thought of James 4:1 (NKJV):

> Where do wars and fights come from among you? Do they not come from your desires for pleasure that war in your members?

The basic instinct to look out for number one is pretty strong. The Bible calls it our sin nature. A lot of fights come from this old nature that is in all of us.

It is a natural instinct for a child to be selfish. He has to be taught to be considerate and thoughtful. Some children (as well as adults) are more sensitive than others to the feelings of other people. This is why some children can be very cruel to another child who may be handicapped or different. They don't stop to think how the other child feels. They are so totally engrossed in their own worlds. This is where we as parents can take the lead.

One day one of our children came home with a note from the bus driver saying that our son had teased a girl on the bus and hurt her feelings. Our son didn't even seem aware of how the girl felt. After we had a long talk in which we said, "How would *you* feel if someone said that to *you?*" he realized that he shouldn't have said what he had, and felt badly about it. He apologized to the girl and then copied James 4 by hand and studied it.

Here are some special problems to watch for in children.

1. *The Instigator.* When this particular child walks into a room it's like letting a fox loose in the henhouse. You hear the ruckus and you *know* who's doing it! This requires firmness on your part and an objective treatment. Remove him from the situation to his room or give him a "time out." I have observed that the "Instigator" is usually looking for attention. He probably feels a bit jealous. Your natural feeling may be a desire to "hit him on the head with a broom" or some other specific treatment! Of course, he *will* get attention—but not the kind that will correct his behavior and shape his character the way you want it shaped. Some children want attention—even negative attention—so badly that they will misbehave to get it.

2. *The Tattler.* Some children tattle a lot because it works for them. The "Tattler" usually feels inadequate, so to make up for it he gets his "heavy"—usually Mom. Mom often is unwittingly being used—she doesn't even know it. *It is best*

to stay out of children's quarrels. Exceptions would be a major infraction of the family rules, or if one child has obviously greatly wronged another child. But when it's just "fussin' and feudin'," take the crying child (usually the younger one!) in your arms, comfort him, and have him stay with you awhile. Then it usually blows over. You can talk to the older child privately later if you feel the situation warrants it. But if, when your child comes crying to you, you always take up his defense, you are setting a precedent that will eventually wear you out. Besides, your children won't learn to solve their own problems.

Be sure that you and your husband reinforce each other as parents. To be a team, you must basically agree and support each other. (See Question #18 on Child Discipline for further information on teamwork.)

RESOURCES

Raising Brothers and Sisters Without Raising the Roof. Carole and Andrew Calladine. Winston Press, 1979.

Sanity in the Summertime. Linda Dillow and Claudia Arp. Thomas Nelson Publishers, 1981.

How to Really Love Your Child. D. Ross Campbell. Victor Books, 1977.

The Idea Book for Mothers. Pat Hershey Owen. Tyndale, 1981.

QUESTION 23

Our teenager has a rebellious attitude. How do we break through to him?

"Rebellious teen" means different things to different people. It may mean a 15-year-old girl wanting to wear more makeup than her parents think she should. It may mean a 17-year-old boy refusing to abide by a curfew and smoking behind his parents' backs. Or it may mean a 13-year-old who is "mouthing off" to his parents and teachers.

Teenagers are children in transition—boys in men's bodies and girls in women's bodies. They are going through enormous changes physically, emotionally, and mentally. They are trying desperately to adjust to their new status as independent, grown-up people. It is exhilarating one moment, disastrous the next.

Do you remember being a teen? When you are feeling frustrated with your teen, sit down and try to remember what you felt like when you were a teenager. Of course your child's world is different from the one you lived in, but the feelings are much the same. You feel as if you are teetering on the edge of the world, excited and scared at the same time. The questions are looming: Will I be popular in school? Whom will I date? Where will I go to college—if I go? Whom shall I marry? What should I be?

Teenagers rebel because they are trying to establish the fact that they are individuals separate from their parents. It's their "Declaration of Independence." Some teenagers make their "declaration" a bit more dramatically than others! Part of this depends on the child's personality and part reflects the parents' style of parenting. If the parents tend to overreact to their children, or try to keep an authoritarian hold on their children even when they are teens ("You do it because I say so"), or fail to convey respect of the teen, teenagers seem to have more of a rebellious attitude.

Dr. James Dobson believes that the need of early adolescents (ages 13 to 14) is to be respected and granted dignity by their parents and to be accepted by their peer group.

Dr. Dobson says, "The most common mistake made by parents of 'older' (16-19) teens is in refusing to grant them the independence and maturity they require."[1]

Love demands freedom; we *must* step back and see our "grown-up" children in a fresh light.

The teen years can really be enjoyable years, in spite of the challenges. We can begin enjoying our children's developing personalities and listen to their opinions and dreams of the future.

Recently as I was cutting my 16-year-old's hair he began telling me of his plans for Bible school, what kind of wife he wanted to find, and his dreams of becoming a missionary. These thoughts he was sharing with me were beautiful, but my internal reaction surprised me: "Wait a minute! You're too young to be saying these kinds of things!" But of course he was not. Growing up is scary for the parents, too. Maybe the reason we have a hard time letting go is because we want to keep our children "ours." But the tighter we hang onto our children, the more they will struggle to be free of us.

Although a teenager is begging for independence, he or she still needs firm guidelines. This is the time to lovingly and consistently give your teen basic guidelines, all the while giving him or her more freedom within those guidelines to make decisions.

If there is a particular behavior that is really bugging you in your child, don't nag him about it. Set a particular time when both parents can sit down and, in a nonaccusing, loving, firm manner, *write out* a few basic guidelines. This may be in regard to a change in attitude that you would like to see, or accountability, or responsibility, etc. Emphasize the fact that you realize he or she is growing up and will be having to make all kinds of decisions on his own. Let your child know that you care very deeply about the direction he is going in life and that you want to help steer him along the right path.

Encourage honest feelings from your teenager. Young people are going through a torrent of emotions at this time in their lives, and they need to feel they can talk to you without threat. It is a tremendous emotional release for them if they can "unload" on you once in a while. Besides, it encourages a feeling of love and trust in you as a parent.

When I was 15 I had horrible, agonizing doubts that God was really *there.* I had been raised in church by godly parents, and though I tried to put aside these doubts, I was inwardly tormented for over a year without verbalizing these thoughts to anyone. One day while my mother and I were doing the dishes, I blurted out my worries. I will never forget my mother's reaction. She laughed and gave me a quick hug. "Honey," she said, "it's all right to question. What good is anything if you can't question it? God is a big God—He can withstand our questions." It wasn't so much her answer as her warm, accepting response of *what* I was feeling that was so reassuring.

If my mother had reacted in horror or shock to my confession, I would have felt that my emotions were all the more something to worry about. There are special moments with your children—*receptive moments*—that you must learn to recognize. *Be ready to listen when they're ready to talk!*

Dr. Ross Campbell, author of *How to Really Love Your Teenager,* believes that it is extremely important that our teens be free to vent their feelings of anger, and that parents allow their teens to express their anger constructively. He believes that the practice of making teens subvert their anger encourages *passive/aggressive* anger. This type of anger gets back at a person (usually the parent) indirectly in forms of procrastination, stubbornness, forgetfulness, and intentional inefficiency.[2]

Above all, show your teenagers that you love them. Here are some specific ways.

1. *Be real.* Share your spiritual victories as well as your personal defeats. Let them *see* your Christianity. Your faith is more readily "caught than taught."

2. *Try to find time alone with your teenager occasionally.* He needs you now more than ever. If your schedule is too hectic and you're trying to make him "fit in" but it's just not working, reexamine your priorities and strip out those things that are nonessential. These are critical years for your child.

3. *Pray for your teenager.* Pray with him before he goes out the door and before he goes to sleep at night. Ask, "Is there anything I can be praying with you about today?" He will appreciate it!

4. *Touch him.* Teens don't understand everything they are going through and sometimes suffer personal anxiety and insecurity. This is where we parents can provide a soothing, reassuring touch. *Physically* touch your teen— hugging is healthy! (Unless you are dropping him off at school—then he would be humiliated!) My oldest son frequently asks to have his back scratched. It's a good time to give that reassuring touch.

Don't worry about being the perfect parent! Relax and have fun with your children. We can't make them perfect. *We're* not! Learn to enjoy them as people.

I remember attending a conference years ago where my husband was the speaker. We had taken our three young children along and I was sitting in the back row with them, trying to keep everything cool. I was beginning to believe I really should have stayed home when a kindly older gentleman sat beside us on the pew and struck up a conversation. I knew of him; he was a minister in our state, and his wife had recently died of cancer. They had had eight beautiful children, now all grown. He smiled at me, "You remind me of my wife when we were young. She always had to sit in the back with the kids because I was in the pulpit." Then he leaned over and offered a bit of advice. "Listen. All the stuff you read on how to do this, how to do that—raising kids isn't that hard! You just have to love 'em, that's all. *Just love 'em.*"

Sometimes in our well-read society we suffer more anxieties than we should because we know there are ways to protect our children's self-esteem, encourage creativity, promote communication, ad infinitum. I believe we must be careful about getting too "processed," thereby losing the joy and spontaneity in life that God intended for us to have. He came to give us life and "life more abundantly." And He promised to make us the "joyful mothers of children" (Psalm 113:9).

RESOURCES

Preparing for Adolescence. James Dobson. Vision House Publishers, 1978.

How to Really Love Your Teenager. D. Ross Campbell. Victor Books, 1981.

Parents and Teenagers. Jay Kesler. Victor Books, 1984.

You Try Being A Teenager: A Challenge to Parents to Understand. Earl D. Wilson. Multnomah Press, 1982.

Adolescence Is Not an Illness. Bruce Narramore, Ph.D. Fleming H. Revell, 1980.

NOTES

1. *Preparing for Adolescence.* James Dobson. Vision House Publishers, 1978.
2. *How to Really Love Your Teenager.* D. Ross Campbell. Victor Books, 1981.

QUESTION 24

> ## My child is handicapped. Do you have any resources that can help?

The most encouraging words I can offer are taken from the Bible: "Come unto Me, all you who labor and are heavy laden, and I will give you rest. Take My yoke upon you and learn from Me, for I am gentle and lowly in heart, and you will find rest for your souls. For My yoke is easy and My burden is light" (Matthew 11:28-30 NKJV).

"Seeing then that we have a great High Priest who has passed through the heavens, Jesus the Son of God, let us hold fast our confession. For we do not have a High Priest who cannot sympathize with our weaknesses, but was in all points tempted as we are, yet without sin. Let us therefore come boldly to the throne of grace, that we may obtain mercy and find grace to help in time of need" (Hebrews 4:14-16 NKJV).

"Surely He has borne our griefs and carried our sorrows. . ." (Isaiah 53:4 NKJV).

As the parent, you have a special kind of burden when you have a handicapped child. But to put this in perspective, we *all* have a handicap of some kind! Some of us put up with a weight problem, a bad back, poor eyesight, allergies, etc. Your child's handicap may weigh heavily upon you, however, as you ponder his future.

It is critically important how you and your family perceive your child. Diane Nason, mother of several handicapped children and author of *Celebration Family,* says, "It is imperative to see *the child* rather than the child who happens

141

to have a handicap." Your emotional ability to deal with the handicap will greatly determine whether your child can develop to his fullest potential.

How prone we are in our culture to label people! Instead of my friend *Susie,* she becomes my friend *Susie-with-cancer.* Instead of seeing *John,* we see him as *John-the-paraplegic.* The handicap overwhelms our image of the real person. We take this kind of reasoning to the other extreme, too. Because of the value we place on money, ability, and prestige, people become Jerry-the-millionaire, my neighbor-who's-president-of-the-company, Sally-the-doctor, and so on.

Dr. Mark Batshaw in his book *The Handicapped Child* details the emotional impact a handicapped child may have on the family.

It is normal to experience grief when you realize your child is handicapped. The loss you feel is for the normal child you had hoped to have. Elisabeth Kubler-Ross has superbly detailed stages of grief in her book *On Death and Dying.* The first stage is usually one of *shock:* "This can't be happening to my child." The next stage may be one of *denial:* "We'll just proceed as if this weren't true." Dr. Batshaw says that parents often experience relief when an older child is diagnosed as being handicapped because they have suspected something was wrong and it is a relief to have it identified.

Parents of handicapped children usually experience *anger:* "Why us?" They may become angry at God, each other, the doctor, and even the child. Anger toward the child, however, usually produces more guilt feelings. If the parents turn their anger inward, they may become depressed, which hinders their ability to cope with the child's handicap.

They also experience *guilt.* Mothers worry that they may have hurt the child somehow during pregnancy. Parents may also feel *isolated* and worry about their feelings toward their child. They may hesitate to express those feelings for fear they will be harshly judged or misunderstood. As in any kind of grieving, it is essential that parents be able to express these feelings to someone who will offer nonjudgmental, unconditional love and support. They desperately need to feel reassurance at this time in their life.

Following this, parents may go through a *bargaining* stage: "If only we can get Joshua to talk" or "If we can just teach Angie to walk"—then everything will be all right. In this bargaining stage, some parents may "intellectualize"—gather factual terms. This could be an effort to protect themselves from their own pain and avoid dealing with their emotions.

Acceptance is the final stage of grief, in which reality is faced. In this stage parents are better equipped to receive information about their child's prognosis, are able to accept the child for who he is, and can also appreciate their own needs. Dr. Batshaw believes that many parents never move beyond the bargaining stage into acceptance, however.[1]

Remember, our High Priest is *touched* by the feeling of our infirmities, and He has carried our sorrows. "He shall feed his flock like a shepherd; he shall gather the lambs with his arms, and carry them in his bosom, and shall gently lead those that are with young" (Isaiah 40:11).

Having a handicapped child may add severe stress to your marriage. You must be able to support each other and take time to regularly communicate. The other children in your family are also affected by having a handicapped brother or sister. Some children secretly worry that they may "catch" the handicap, or may feel "glad it's not them" who is retarded. Resentment may also build because the parents have to devote a great deal of time to the handicapped child, leaving little time for the other family members. Your children need to have an outlet for their feelings, and you can help to draw them out with loving awareness and consistent encouragement.

Actually, most children who have handicapped siblings develop a greater sensitivity, compassion, and understanding for the handicapped.

When I was a freshman in high school, a classmate of mine gave a talk in speech class about her brother, who had Downs syndrome. She explained it well and told of his accomplishments with pride. We all knew she had a "retarded" brother but didn't talk much about it for fear we would embarrass her. From that time on Tommy was special to all of us because the fear of his handicap was erased and we saw him just for his delightful self.

Encourage your child to live up to his fullest potential, whatever that may be. His future can be bright and full of promise.

RESOURCES

Celebration Family. Diane Nason with Birdie Etchison. Thomas Nelson Publishers, 1983.

We Have Been There. Compiled by Dougan, Isbell, and Ayas. Abingdon, 1979.

A Step Further. Joni Eareckson and Steve Estes. Zondervan, 1978.

Of Braces and Blessings. Bonnie G. Wheeler. Christian Herald Books, 1980.

NOTES

1. *The Handicapped Child.* Dr. Mark Batshaw. Paul H. Brooks Publishing Co.

QUESTION 25

> *I think I'm abusing my children.*
> *Please help me.*

Look at this scenario and see if it fits your typical pattern.

You find yourself worn-out, unhappy, or discouraged. Problems and tensions seem to be mounting in your life, and you are frequently irritated.

Then there's the straw that breaks the camel's back. Your child's crying, misbehavior, or attitude sends your emotions cascading over the top. You feel the anger rising inside you, and you feel like you're losing control.

Your blood starts pumping, you feel your jaw tighten, your breathing increases, and your grip on whatever is at hand makes your knuckles white.

For a split second, you try to control yourself. Something inside tries to tell you to calm down, but your anger and frustration take over.

At that moment you begin to slap, hit, or scream at your child.

Later you try to rationalize your behavior by saying that your child was in fact misbehaving and that you had warned or told him or her "a hundred times before" not to do that. But inside you are filled with guilt and remorse because you know your reaction was wrong and more severe than the offense.

If this sounds like the occasional you, you may be abusing your child or at least have the capability of child abuse. You are not alone. Many parents, at certain times, lose control.

145

Often these feelings have little to do with our child's misbehavior. Sometimes they can be traced to our childhood and our own feelings of low self-esteem. At other times they are by-products of mounting stress and tension that have been hidden inside because we haven't found an acceptable way to vent our feelings.

Christians are especially vulnerable to this because we are often told to act victorious and to never display any fear, anxiety, anger, or frustration. Because of this we place ourselves under an unusual and unreal amount of stress. Yet the Bible offers concrete keys to overcoming child abuse.

Here are some guidelines that can help you overcome being a child-abuser or potential child-abuser.

1. *Realize that you are human.* Just because you are a Christian does not mean that you never get tired or irritable or that the pressures of life do not affect your emotions. God's Word says that we can admit (in fact, *should* admit) that we are weak within ourselves. David the psalmist cried out to God, "Pity me, O Lord, for I am weak. Heal me, for my body is sick and I am upset and disturbed. My mind is filled with apprehension and gloom. Oh, restore me soon" (Psalm 6:2,3 TLB).

You are not the only Christian who experiences bouts with anger and rage. When we admit our weaknesses and inadequacies, we can take heart because, as the apostle Paul says in 2 Corinthians 12:10, "When I am weak, then I am strong." It is our dependence upon God that will lead to victory over the uncontrollable feelings and frustrations within.

2. *Get in touch with your feelings.* While it can become obsessive and sometimes unhealthy to constantly look inward, it is important for us to be in touch with our feelings in an effort to better understand some of our behavior. Rarely does anger, resentment, or rage toward our children result in the fact that we hate our kids. In fact, the opposite is generally true. We love our kids more than anything! And that makes our guilt over abuse even more painful. More often it is because we dislike *ourselves.* Our self-dislike and

hatred is expressed toward other people. Sometimes our anger arises because of an unusual amount of stress. Marriage, job, finances, depression, discontentment, or feelings of resentment can all add to the situation.

Ask God to reveal your emotions to you. David said in Psalm 139:1-4, "O Lord, thou has searched me and known me. Thou knowest my downsitting and mine uprising; thou understandest my thought afar off. Thou compassest my path and my lying down, and art acquainted with all my ways. For there is not a word in my tongue, but, lo, O Lord, thou knowest it altogether."

Realize that God knows the inner you and can help you understand your own emotions and responses. Recognize that your child's behavior at that moment of potential eruption is *not* the true source of these monstrous feelings inside you. You can train your mind and heart to remember that the child's behavior is not the sole cause. Remember that if you feel great anger or rage, you may overreact to the situation.

3. *Resist taking any immediate action.* Wait until you have sorted through your emotions and the situation. It is important for you to be in control of yourself *before* making any disciplinary response to your child's behavior.

You have heard the proverbial "count to ten." Rita Bennett in her book *I'm Glad You Asked That* (Fleming H. Revell, 1983) says she has a better method. "Count to nine by naming the nine fruits of the Holy Spirit," says Rita. "I started counting with the first fruit, love, and that's as far as I needed to count."

4. *Pray.* Paul in Philippians 4:6,7 states, "Don't worry about anything; instead, pray about everything; tell God your needs and don't forget to thank him for his answers. If you do this you will experience God's peace, which is far more wonderful than the human mind can understand. His peace will keep your thoughts and your hearts quiet and at rest as you trust in Christ Jesus" (TLB).

Stormie Omartian, popular gospel songwriter, singer, and

author, was severely abused by her mother as a child. Her moving story tells of the victorious grace of God. Stormie was locked in a closet until she was six years old and severely abused until she was 12. The scars remained with Stormie into her adult life, until she came to a saving knowledge of Jesus Christ.

After her conversion experience and her Christian walk was well underway, Stormie had her first child. She felt that all the awful hurts of her abusive childhood had been removed by then. One day, though, her infant son was crying in his crib and nothing seemed to calm him. Suddenly Stormie felt a rage within her and an uncontrollable urge to slap her child. She tells how distraught she was at this ugly thing she still found imbedded in her nature. Stormie says that whenever she felt this urge, she immediately left the child's room, went to her own room, fell on her knees, and began to pray.

Nothing can be more effective in curbing anger, irrational response, or potential child abuse than to spend time in prayer before disciplining your child. Stormie Omartian says that this was a key to her ability in overcoming potential abuse.

5. *Determine a rational course of action.* Discipline is not wrong if a child needs correction. Spanking or some other form of corrective discipline is acceptable when you are in control and are acting out of love. Learn to recognize the difference between discipline and punishment. God will give you wisdom on how to discipline your child as you *wait* on Him. *Never* discipline your child in anger. Always discipline from a viewpoint of corrective, redemptive love. Then be quick to forgive and to restore your child into your full acceptance.

6. *Reach out to someone.* In today's society, the traditional support system of family ties and close friendships is often disrupted due in part to our extreme mobility. This often leaves men and women feeling alone and isolated, with no one to whom they can turn.

Sometimes we feel ashamed or afraid to tell anyone (pastor, husband, or close friend) about our problems for fear of their response and possible rejection of us. Yet it is vital that we share our burden with someone we trust so that they can help and encourage us. Involve yourself in a Bible study or prayer group for added support and encouragement. Many times your "trusted friend" can come out of these groups.

If you or someone you know is having a problem of severe abuse (beating a child to the point of bruising, bleeding, or broken bones; sexually abusing a child; severely emotionally abusing a child, such as locking him in a closet; or torturing a child) professional help should be sought at once. Call a pastor or another trusted counselor so that he can give the necessary counsel and support in overcoming this problem. For further help and advice, here are some numbers you can call to talk with people who care, will keep your confidence, and will listen to you:

PARENTS ANONYMOUS

1 (800) 421-0353   1 (800) 352-0386
(outside California)   (California only)

CHILD HELP USA   1 (800) 422-4453

RESOURCES

Out of Control. Kathy C. Miller. Word Books, 1984.

QUESTION 26_____

I need information about sexual abuse of children.

Sexual abuse of children is a delicate topic of discussion in Christian circles. While this type of abuse has no doubt been going on for ages, it has been unthinkable to the Christian community that this problem exists within Christian families with any significance or regularity.

The Christian community was shocked recently when a popular Christian doctor/writer was arrested and charged with aggravated sodomy with a 14-year-old girl.

Statistics tell us that an estimated one of every five girls has experienced some form of sexual abuse, most often with a close relative. In fact, the old idea that this behavior is generally carried out by "perverts" and "dirty old men" has been proved false. Child-molesters often appear quite respectable, relatively young, and frequently known to the victim. A full three-fourths of them are friends, relatives, and neighbors.

There are few statistics to indicate how prevalent incest and other forms of child sexual abuse are within church-related families, but, like all forms of sin, it does exist, and the church has all too often been silent about it. The Bible states that "the heart is desperately wicked—who can know it?" If the churches are reaching out to their communities with help and caring, they will encounter sexually abused children.

Maybe you know of a situation where you suspect incest or child abuse. Maybe you are in a family relationship where this is happening, or maybe you simply want to educate your children on how to avoid being a victim.

In any case, in order to detect or educate people about child sexual abuse, we must be willing to admit that the problem does exist in all strata of our society, including the churches. We can no longer treat a child as "exaggerating" when telling someone about a problem of this nature, nor can we simply say "so-and-so would *never* do such a thing." Here are some guidelines that we hope will help.

1. *Identifying the victims.* There are several traits to look for when trying to determine whether a child has in fact been sexually abused.

First, children seldom lie about such matters. *Newsweek* magazine, May 14, 1984, reported:

> "We have a very long intellectual tradition that discredits the testimony of women and children when they complain about sexual assault," says Harvard Medical School psychiatrist Judith Herman. False charges are rare, she insists. "More commonly there are false retractions of true complaints" after a child gives in to family pressure not to testify against an abusive relative. Child advocates won't deny that children invent tales sometimes. But attorney David Lloyd of Washington's Children's Hospital has a simple test: "Listen for details the child would not know if he or she had not witnessed sexual conduct." Children simply don't fantasize about perverted adult behaviors.

Second, children will often demonstrate changes in behavior or unusual fears. A child may withdraw and become less verbal. Or a child may begin to show signs of living in a fantasy world in order to escape reality. In still other cases, the child may suddenly demonstrate fear toward certain adults or cling to her mother or other trusted adult. Often the child can become rebellious or manipulative. Any sudden changes in behavior patterns, especially coupled with other signs or circumstances, may indicate sexual abuse.

If a child suddenly refuses to be left alone with a particular babysitter or relative, try to discover why the child has developed this new fear. It could simply be a reluctance to want to leave you, or it could be an indication of a problem. Sometimes a child will demonstrate a sudden new degree of sexual behavior or knowledge, such as seductive behavior, gestures, or conversation of a sexual nature. While being careful not to appear shocked, try to discover the origin of such behavior or knowledge.

2. *Educating your child.* For years we have all warned our children not to accept candy or rides from strangers. But this is not enough. Children need to be educated on how they can understand and combat sexual abuse.

First, teach your child that it is all right to say *no* to an adult. Children, especially from conservative homes, have been taught to be respectful and obedient to adults and to be quiet when told to be quiet. This can inadvertently prepare them to be perfect victims. Instead, children should understand that there are certain things that no adult—even a relative—has a right to ask for or do to a child. A parent/child workbook titled *Little Ones' Activity Workbook,* by Lynn Heitritter, is an excellent learning tool in teaching your children protection from sexual abuse. It is written from a Christian perspective and does an excellent job of teaching a child the difference between a "No" touch and a healthy-relationship "Yes" touch.

Second, begin to rely more on your intuition and instincts. When you sense that your child feels uncomfortable with hugs and kisses from certain relatives or friends, respect the child's feelings instead of insisting that she "kiss Uncle Pete good-bye," etc.

Third, encourage your child to yell or scream and to run to a nearby house or trusted adult when feeling in danger of sexual abuse.

Fourth, encourage your child to tell you *everything.* Reassure him or her that you are a caring friend who will not be offended or shocked by his or her discussions. Every child needs some trusted adult that he or she feels comfortable in telling secrets to.

Fifth, teach your children that it's not their fault if something happens. Often children who have experienced an incestuous relationship feel guilt over the potential breakup of the home. Somehow kids transfer the blame for the event onto themselves, and this leads to denial or reluctance to tell anyone about it. Teach your child even before it happens that things of this nature are accidents in which they are the victim, much like getting hit by an object or breaking a bone.

Nothing beats maintaining a close personal relationship with your child. If your child has already been a victim, trust the Lord to heal your child's memories. Pray with your child, show acceptance and trust, and let God do the healing process.

RESOURCES

Little Ones' Activity Workbook. Lynn Heitritter. P.O. Box 725, Young America, Minnesota 55399.

PARENTS ANONYMOUS

1 (800) 421-0353
(outside California)

1 (800) 352-0386
(California only)

CHILD HELP USA

1 (800) 422-4453

Part VI

Pregnancy

QUESTION 27

We've tried, but I can't seem to get pregnant. What should we do?

Unfortunately, infertility is an agonizing problem for many couples today. Some authorities estimate that 15 percent of all married couples are infertile. Other estimates put infertility as high as one couple in five who can't get pregnant within a year. Making infertility even more difficult to handle is the insensitive way in which couples are often treated by others who have no idea of the anguish the couple is experiencing. A friend who was not able to conceive a child tells of going to baby shower after baby shower, only to hear comments like, "Hey, when is it *your* turn?" or "When are you two going to get with it and have a baby?" The panic grows as the years go by and there is still no baby. Reading daily accounts in the newspaper of abused, abandoned children and the high rate of abortion only rubs more salt in the wound. It doesn't seem fair: *Why us?* We have so much love to give, and yet we can't conceive.

The barren womb is not a new problem. Sarah finally conceived in later years and bore Isaac. Then there was Rachel, the second wife of Jacob, who finally did have two sons. These women tried all sorts of alternate methods to satisfy the ache of empty arms: They went so far as to use their maids to produce children. Rachel wanted to try eating mandrakes (we would call them tomatoes), which were believed to aid pregnancy. Proverbs 30:15,16 says there are four things which are never satisfied, among them a barren womb.

People who seem to be infertile still "try things" these days. The good news is that with new developments in medical science, many couples are able to have children. What actually causes infertility? First of all, let's discuss what factors are necessary to conceive.

1. The male must produce a sufficient number of normal, live sperm.

2. The female must produce a healthy egg (ovum), must ovulate, and must release the egg from the ovaries into the Fallopian tubes.

3. The tubes must be open so the egg can find its way down into the uterus.

4. The sperm must be able to pass from the testicles, where they are formed, out through the penis at the time of ejaculation.

5. The male must be able to ejaculate and deposit the sperm in the vagina.

6. The sperm must travel up through the cervix into the uterus and on out the Fallopian tubes.

7. If ovulation has occurred and an egg is present, the sperm must be able to penetrate and fertilize the egg.

8. The reproductive organs of the woman must be prepared to receive the sperm and allow it to migrate from the vagina through the cervix and into the tube.

9. The organs must be healthy and able to nourish the sperm in its passage to the egg, and they must also be capable of protecting and nourishing the fertilized egg to full development.

10. The fertilized egg must attach itself to the wall of the uterus.

11. Normal development must then take place at each stage to avoid rejection (miscarriage).

If there is a problem anywhere in this chain of events, infertility can result. Here are some of the problems that may cause infertility.

1. The husband may be infertile because a) he has an insufficient number of sperm, b) the sperm are not moving

fast enough, or c) he has blocked passageways. There are several things that could have caused this to happen to him: disease, infections, fevers, or congenital abnormalities.

2. Most women who are infertile have problems with the functions of the various parts of the reproductive tract: a) She may not be ovulating; b) the uterus may not be properly prepared to receive the fertilized egg; c) the Fallopian tubes may be blocked, diseased, or bound by adhesions; d) the cervix may not produce an adequate amount of mucus favorable to the reception and migration of the sperm. Other problems in the female could be disease, infections, problem with hormone production, and congenital abnormalities. Obesity, poor nutrition, stress, excessive smoking, and excessive alcohol intake have also been linked to infertility problems.

What can be done to rectify the problem of infertility? It is important for *both* husband and wife to have a complete physical examination by a doctor with knowledge of infertility problems. This will be a time-consuming and tedious process, and the couple must be prepared to fully cooperate with the doctor. It will take commitment, patience, and a determination not to get discouraged as they try to find exactly what is causing the problem.

The couple will also be asked questions about their sexual relations to see if their infertility may be related to such factors as timing or frequency of intercourse. Often a couple may simply need more information on the sexual techniques that are most favorable to conception. A medical history will be taken of the woman to see if there were any illnesses (such as appendicitis or gonorrhea) which may have damaged her reproductive organs.

The husband is usually asked to bring a sample of his semen into a laboratory. The sample will be analyzed to get a sperm count and to see how healthy the sperm are. Other factors will also be analyzed.

Because the woman's reproductive system is more complex than the man's, she will probably have more testing.

To determine whether ovulation has occurred is done by evaluating a record of the woman's basal body temperature. For this study the woman takes her temperature every morning upon awakening and records her temperature before getting out of bed. A record usually has to be kept for a two- to three-month period. The record is not for planning the time of intercourse but is for the physician to determine if ovulation has been occurring.

There are several methods to see if at least one of the Fallopian tubes is open. One method is attempting to pass carbon dioxide gas through the tubes. By observing pressure changes, it is possible to determine whether the tube is open. This procedure is usually performed in the doctor's office.

Another method uses X-rays and is usually done in a radiologist's office or the X-ray department of a hospital. A dye is injected into the uterus and an X-ray is taken. This not only tells whether the tubes are open but also outlines the shape of the uterus.

The Fallopian tubes may also be observed through a laparoscopic examination. This technique permits the physician to look into the abdomen and inspect the various organs, including the female organs. This is usually done under general anesthetic and on an outpatient basis. The laparoscope, a miniature telescope with a lens and a lighting system, is inserted through a small incision (½ inch or less) at the lower edge of the navel. The presence of any pelvic disease which may interfere with conception can be determined. Also, it is usually possible to tell whether an operation is necessary or whether an operation to correct significant problems will offer a reasonable chance of success.

Another factor, which is a relatively new discovery, is the possibility of sperm antibodies. If present, antibodies may prevent conception by attacking and destroying sperm, even as other types of antibodies in the body attack bacteria. The presence of such antibodies and their effect on conception is still not entirely clear, but more is being learned about this.

It is also possible for the doctor to take several specimens of semen (if the count is low) and concentrate it for successful insemination.

If the semen analysis shows that there are too few sperm being produced, or do not have sufficient motility, then further investigation of that specific problem is done. This is usually done by a urologist, and the treatment depends upon the specific problem.

If the evaluation shows that the woman is not ovulating, she may be helped by taking one of the "infertility" drugs. In certain cases surgery may be performed in an effort to establish ovulation, to enlarge a closed cervix, to open blocked tubes, or to remove diseased tissue in the lining of the uterus.

What about artificial insemination? There are from 100,000 to 500,000 children in the United States who were produced by using artificial insemination. Live male sperm is inseminated into the uterus. This procedure of artificial insemination is routinely done by infertility specialists for couples who wish to conceive. It requires an average of three inseminations before pregnancy results.

At first glance this may seem to be the perfect solution to infertility if the husband has the problem. Because of the high rate of abortion and the fact that unwed mothers are keeping their babies, adoption of healthy infants has become difficult. Hence the attractiveness of artificial insemination.

However, artificial insemination (using a donor other than the husband) raises serious ethical and moral questions:

— Is it proper to allow a doctor to name the husband as the father, when he is not?
— Is artificial insemination (using a donor) a form of adultery?
— Does artificial insemination fall within God-ordained procreation in marriage?
— What about the moral responsibilities of the donor and doctor?

In vitro fertilization is another practice that is helping some infertile couples. It too raises many questions. *In vitro* means fertilizing a mother's egg outside her body, then having it implanted back in the womb. The ban against in vitro fertilization has been lifted in the United States by the Department of Health, Education and Welfare, with certain restrictions: Embryos can only be formed from sperm and eggs of "lawfully married couples." Experimentation must be done only during the first 14 days after fertilization, and the public must be told of any evidence that in vitro produces a higher number of abnormal fetuses.

Most fertilization techniques are new. The moral/ethical questions are yet to be worked out, and a great amount of caution and discernment needs to be exercised.

If you cannot have children for whatever reason, we encourage you to prayerfully consider God's plan for your family. There are many alternatives, some with rather profound overriding questions. Hopefully the Christian community will continue to offer positive help in making your decision.

RESOURCES

Intended for Pleasure. Ed and Gaye Wheat. Fleming H. Revell, 1981.
Life In The Balance. James C. Hefley. Victor Books, 1980.

QUESTION 28

> ## I've just had a miscarriage. Can you help me cope?

Over 300,000 women in America suffer miscarriages every year. That represents approximately one out of every five normal full-term pregnancies.

Cold statistics don't mean much, however, when it happens to *you*. Losing a baby due to miscarriage is a very real loss. Mari Hanes in her book *Beyond Heartache* (Tyndale, 1984) says that after having a miscarriage a woman's "body screams to her that it is no longer pregnant. Jolted back to an unpregnant state, it works to normalize hormone levels and the entire reproductive system. For weeks her physical form has been 'home' for someone else. Now internal organs such as the pituitary gland flood her body with one message: 'vacant.' "

It may help you to know some facts and myths about miscarriage. This information has been adapted from an article by Karleen Jackson in the May/June 1983 issue of *Virtue* magazine. Here are the major causes of miscarriage.

1. *Problems with the baby.* Most babies that have been miscarried, when closely examined, were found to be physically defective in some way. This may be the result of genetic mistakes or some infection (such as rubella) which disrupts the development of the baby.

2. *Problems with where the fertilized ovum becomes implanted.* Occasionally implantation will occur in the Fallopian tube or near the mouth of the cervix, making it impossible for the pregnancy to develop properly.

163

3. *Infections.* Recent studies show that some bacterial infections, such as mycoplasma infection, can cause miscarriage. Treatment for this infection is readily available.

4. *Problems with the uterus or cervix.* Fibroid tumors, an unusually shaped uterus, or a weakened cervix can lead to miscarriage. (Anatomical abnormalities, however, can often be surgically corrected.)

5. *Improper care or nutrition for the mother.* Studies show that women who are diabetic or who have dealt with anorexia nervosa may be more likely to have a miscarriage. Adequate nutrition and medical care are essential to normal pregnancy.

Here are some common myths about miscarriage.

1. *An accident I suffered must have caused my miscarriage.* Sherwin A. Kaufman, M.D., states, "A well-implanted egg with firm moorings in the uterus has been likened to a healthy unripened apple on the tree: a fresh gust of wind will not cause it to fall."[1]

2. *Sexual relations early in my pregnancy must have caused my miscarriage.* Dr. Kaufman further says, "If miscarriages were caused by intercourse, the birth rate would drop to zero. Despite a common and persistent belief that coitus is somehow harmful to pregnancy, there is no scientific evidence to support this."

3. *Strenuous exercise must have caused my miscarriage.* To quote Dr. Kaufman further, "Contrary to belief, ordinary (and even extraordinary) activity does not cause miscarriage."

As stated earlier, a miscarriage is a genuine loss. Because miscarriage involves the death of a loved one, there is a need for the woman who has miscarried and her family to grieve. This fact is sometimes overlooked.

Realize that grief is a process which has several recognizable steps that commonly occur. Elisabeth Kubler-Ross, M.D., in her book *On Death and Dying* lists five stages of grief:

1. Denial and isolation
2. Anger

3. Bargaining
4. Depression
5. Acceptance

Sometimes these steps are gone through quickly; some may not seem to be experienced at all, and some may be repeated before the final stage of acceptance is achieved. Recognizing the grief process makes it easier to deal with each step as it is reached.

Karleen Jackson tells her personal experience of emotional healing after miscarriage:

> . . . About two weeks later I began to feel that God couldn't bring anything good out of this tragedy. Although I put on a brave front, appearing to be in control, I had burrowed into a bottomless pit of guilt and depression.
>
> My husband, Rich, finally saw through the facade, forcing me to voice my misery. Because I couldn't figure out how God could possibly salvage this horrible experience for good, I'd decided He had made His first big mistake. Rich listened to each irrational thought that ushered through my tears, then made a statement that had tremendous impact on my heart: "Let God be God."
>
> The next day I read in Isaiah 55:8,9, " 'For my thoughts are not your thoughts, neither are your ways my ways,' declares the Lord. 'As the heavens are higher than the earth, so are my ways higher than your ways and my thoughts than your thoughts.' " And in Psalm 18:30 I was reminded, "As for God, his way is perfect . . ." (NIV). At long last I released God to be God without having to understand why this experience had happened. From that point on I began to heal emotionally.[2]

Here are some Scriptures to help you realize that God does know and care about the unborn.

> The Lord has called me from the womb; from the matrix of my mother He has made mention of my name (Isaiah 49:1 NKJV).

You have formed my inward parts; You have covered me in my mother's womb. I will praise You, for I am fearfully and wonderfully made; marvelous are Your works, and that my soul knows very well. My frame was not hidden from You, when I was made in secret, and skillfully wrought in the lowest parts of the earth.

Your eyes saw my substance, being yet unformed. And in Your book they all were written, the days fashioned for me, when as yet there were none of them.

How precious also are Your thoughts to me, O God! How great is the sum of them! If I should count them, they would be more in number than the sand; when I awake, I am still with You (Psalm 139:13-18 NKJV).

The loss of a child—even one that is not fully developed—brings pain and sorrow to the parent. What a comfort to know that our God knows about our little ones *intimately*—and He cares!

RESOURCES

Beyond Heartache. Mari Hanes with Jack Hayford. Tyndale, 1984.

NOTES

1. *You Can Have a Baby.* Sherwin A. Kaufman, M.D. Bantam Books, 1980.
2. Karleen Jackson, "Miscarriage: Facts and Myths," in the May/June 1983 issue of *Virtue* magazine.

QUESTION 29

We're considering adopting a child. How can we get started?

Adopting a child today is a challenge, but it can be done. There *are* children today who need parents. Adoptive parents who are prayerfully persistent can see their dream realized, but it will take commitment and determination.

If you desire an infant from the United States, you must face the fact that there are fewer babies available today because of the liberal abortion laws and because many unwed mothers are keeping their babies. However, if you cannot have children biologically or only have one child, you will receive priority over other families.

Prayerfully begin your search. It really is an exciting process—one that involves you as a couple and your entire family. It can also be a discouraging process because what sometimes seems like a hot lead turns into a dead end. Or the child that you thought was to be yours is placed with another family. Finding your child is a walk of faith. You pray for God's wisdom and leading, and then you start weaving your way through the tangle of agencies, red tape, and government bureaucracy to get your child.

Begin by contacting your local agencies, private and public. You will have to do some investigative checking to find an agency best suited to your individual needs. Locate people in your community who have adopted a child and find out what agency they used. It may take you some time to find the right avenue for your particular situation. (It took our family two years to find an agency that could meet our needs.)

167

Once you have found an agency you feel compatible with, you must have a home study. This is essentially an in-depth profile of your family, and it is necessary. It may seem strange to you to be so scrutinized when all you want is a child to love—but it is something that is required. Expect to have definite "labor" pains!

Home study requirements usually involve:

1. One office visit to the agency and two home visits by a social worker.
2. Evidence of financial and medical capability (tax form or financial statement).
3. Personal references.

After you have completed your home study, if that agency is unable to meet your adoption inquiries for children, don't wait! "The squeaky wheel gets the oil." Most agencies have adoption exchange books from various states that contain lists of children who are available for adoption. If your agency does not have the exchange books, ask where the closest contact is to see them.

Ask your agency for names of adoptive parents, parent groups, or pre-adopt groups in your area. These people can be an invaluable source of encouragement to you in the adoption process. At the end of this chapter is suggested reading. *It is very important that you find out as much as you can by reading.* It will help your search.

There are approximately 150,000 children available for adoption right now in the United States. Another 50,000 are in the process of being released for adoption. There are many more children besides these in foster care of institutions. Foster care should exist to provide a temporary home for the child *six months old or less* while his parents are getting it together or the department is getting it apart, legally. But "The System" seems to have created its own monster. Of approximately one-half million children now in foster care, one in four have been in care more than *six years!*

Adoption of "special needs" children is the greatest need

in adoption today. These are children with physical, emotional, or mental handicaps. Often these children have been abused. They also represent children of minority races, biracial children, sibling groups, and older children. Almost all children available today for adoption fall into one or more of these categories.

Dennis and Diane Nason have adopted 32 of these children. They also have six biological children. Their book *Celebration Family* is excellent reading for anyone considering any kind of adoption. They have experienced every kind of adoption imaginable—from healthy infants to Downs syndrome to nine-year-old black/white twins from Harlem. The Nasons are personal friends of ours, and we can vouch for the fact that a "special needs" child gives as much delight and joy as any other.

Diane says:

> When talking of the handicapped child, the usual fear is that of the unknown. This can be erased by accepting the creativity of God, freeing parents of fear. *It is imperative to see a child with a unique personality who happens to have a handicap—instead of just seeing the handicap.* Frequently asked questions in these adoptions are "What will it do to the family?" "Will the family of over-average intelligence have to slow down for a mental handicap?" "Will we have to give up backpacking or horseback riding?" *The fear of the child must be erased,* and the focus be on the family unit working together. Parents who ask for children with handicaps must have a capacity for growth, an understanding of our American cultural myths and the prayerful responsibility of enjoying a child and the purpose unfolding in this unique life. Again, *commitment* is the key word . . . commitment to provide a loving, safe and stable environment for a child. . . commitment to never give up trying to help the child, praying for the child, seeking advice of other parents, professionals, if need be. . . commitment to the Lord to raise that child for however long He asks you to be an intricate part of his life.

Our own family is a transracial family in that we adopted our daughter from another country (Korea). If you decide to go overseas with adoption, be sensitive to the fact that your child will experience cultural shock when he or she arrives home with you. You can imagine what it might be like for your own child if you were to send him from his American culture to a foreign country to live with strangers!

In spite of all the legal tangle, endless papers, and countless fees, adoption is worth it because it brings a precious child home to you. As an anonymous poet put it:

> Not flesh of my flesh, nor bone of my bone,
> But still miraculously my own.
> Never forget for a single minute,
> You didn't grow under my heart...but in it!

RESOURCES

The Adoption Book. Sheila Macmanus. Paulist Press, 1984.

Celebration Family. Diane Nason with Birdie Etchison. Thomas Nelson Publishers, 1983.

The Forever Family: Our Adventures in Adopting Older Children. Ruth Piepenbrink. Our Sunday Visitor, Inc., 1981.

Part VII _____

Organization & Finances

QUESTION 30_____

> ## My husband lost his job, and I feel panicky. What should we do?

Losing your main source of income is an anxiety-filled event. These are turbulent times of economic transition in America. The financial climate is constantly changing, and thousands of families find themselves in the crisis of a layoff.

We sympathize with your situation. It is natural to feel some stress, anxiety, and uncertainty at this time.

Here are several things to consider that will help you get a handle on your circumstances and point you in the right direction.

1. *Sit down together and reassess essentials and nonessentials.* This means to determine what you *can* do without and what you *cannot* do without. Begin by making three lists with the following headings:

Absolute essentials: Such things as tithes, food, rent or house payment, utilities, etc.

Essentials high on our list but not absolute: Such things as payment on second car, payment on piano, expensive gifts, etc.

Nonessentials: Such things as new clothing, entertainment, three-week vacation, long-distance phone calls, etc.

Determine together which expenditures to put on which list. Then eliminate items starting at the bottom of the nonessentials list and working upward. Come up with a realistic budget even if you must cut into the essentials list.

2. *Investigate your unemployment benefits and make sure you are receiving the maximum for which you are entitled.* Also

be sure to find out how long they will last and when they will run out. Be sure to work unemployment benefits into your budget plan.

3. *Learn to live on less.* Even your "absolute essentials" can be reduced, sometimes drastically! Learn to shop for better food buys (cheaper cuts of meat, etc.) and to use less electricity or gas by turning off lights, turning the thermostat down, and wearing a sweater. To save fuel, consolidate trips to town whenever possible, participate in a car pool, or ride the bus. There are no doubt many things you can discover as savings.

4. *Avoid revolving charge accounts.* Nothing is more devastating to your overall financial future than to continue using easy credit. If you have charge cards, now is a good time to *stop using them.* Since your income has been severely cut back, it is far better to cut back your living expenses than it is to "charge it." This could severely financially strap you, even after you return to work. Also avoid short-term, high-interest loans. It is a good way to lose your house, car, or other securities you may pledge to qualify for the loan. Again, while it may provide some temporary relief, it will come back to hurt you later.

5. *If necessary, try to renegotiate long-term debts.* Often a local bank will be quite sympathetic to your situation. Talk to your banker to see if temporarily reduced payments can be arranged for your house, car, etc. If your payment record and credit rating have been good, sometimes the banks will cooperate. After all, the last thing they want is to go through foreclosure proceedings and take back your house or car. This may not work, since all banks are different, but it is certainly worth a try if your needs dictate a cut in monthly payments.

6. *Be willing to take a temporary job or part-time work.* Depending on the laws in your state, you may be able to take some temporary or part-time work and still collect unemployment payments. You should be willing to temporarily take any work that comes along, even if it's not in

your field and pays less than you are worth. After all, the objective is *survival* until you can find the right job.

7. *Learn the blessings of a savings account.* If you have a savings account that you have been systematically contributing to, you know the benefit of being able to fall back on it as a source of income to help tide you over. If you do not have a savings account, now is a good time to make a profound mental impression on yourself so that when things improve again, one of your first priorities will be to start one!

In addition to the preceding seven items, you must learn to cope with your stress.

1. *Losing a job can be ego-shattering.* Often a man's self-esteem is wrapped up in his career. Your husband probably suffers to some degree any or all of several potentially disabling emotions, especially if in his early days of search for a new job he is unsuccessful. These symptoms could include feelings of uselessness, failure, depression, anxiety, anger, frustration, etc. If he is the typical American male, he will do his best to hide his feelings. What he needs from you, his wife, at this point is not "free advice" but affirmation.

Often wives want to help out by giving some advice: "Did you go see so-and-so?" "Did you put your application in here?" "Why don't you try this or try that?" Statements like these tend to antagonize your husband and only deepen his feelings of anxiety. Remember that he has been a good provider and wants to go back to work as much as you want him to. If he's acting paralyzed or listless or uninterested, it is most likely not because he's lazy or disinterested, but because he is suffering discouragement and depression.

The best thing you can do is *affirm* him. Tell him that you love him, that you believe in him, that you trust him, that he has always been a good provider, that he is capable, that his next employer will be lucky to have a man of his caliber, etc. In other words, *supplement his ego at this critical time.* He needs to hear your affirmation that he has value and is a capable person. I can guarantee that this approach will do more for your marriage and be a better motivating factor to your husband than anything else you could do during this crisis.

2. *Leave each other room to breathe.* Often when a layoff hits, your husband is home all day, "under your feet." Your routine becomes as disrupted as his. While he may help you with household chores, he may also begin to give you unasked-for advice on how to do things. He may point out your "wrong way" that has actually worked quite successfully for you over the years.

Be careful not to fall into the trap of getting on each other's nerves. In the July/August 1983 issue of *Virtue* magazine, Martha Lou Farmer states in an article titled "When Lay-Off Strikes Your Marriage," "The smart couple recognizes and allows for the fact that they occasionally have to back off and give each other 'breathing room' in order to keep their marriage fresh and vibrant. Total togetherness can be dangerous. If you've never had an opportunity to discover all the possible areas you may disagree with your mate, this could be it!"

She goes on to say on the positive side that this could also be a good opportunity to discover where you do agree. She concludes by stating that the hazards of "total togetherness" can be minimized by "channeling one's attention to other people and new activities whenever possible."

It is important to give each other time away from each other, or time alone. All of us need space, so agree to back off and give each other some room, especially during this difficult time.

3. *Be honest with each other.* Men have a tendency to gloss over the financial crisis. In an effort to help you not worry so much, he may paint an unrealistically rosy picture. If you as a wife handle the finances, don't hide the fact from him to protect his anxiety. Be honest with each other on exactly how much unemployment compensation there will be, how much is in savings, and how much is being spent. Also be honest with your own feelings so that you can lean on each other for encouragement and moral support.

4. *Communicate to your husband that you cannot be all things to him.* Often when a husband gets laid off, the wife has to go to work (or keep working) and still be wife, mom, cook, housekeeper, and vivacious sex partner. If you add to this the responsibility of being total moral support, it can become overwhelming.

Encourage your husband to seek an outside friend, pastor, or relative to confide in and communicate with. Recognize that you cannot be your husband's sole source of encouragement and support. This is a stressful responsibility that is unfair for you to bear alone.

Let your husband know that you have physical and emotional limits, and ask him for the help you need to cope.

Of supreme importance to all of us is to remember who our true Source is. A job is not your source, nor is a paycheck or bank account. *God* is your Source.

David the psalmist said, after observing life for many years in all sorts of crises, "I have been young, and now am old, yet have I not see the righteous forsaken, nor his children begging bread" (Psalm 37:25). Jesus, in attempting to teach us lessons of trust, used the simple elements of grass, lilies, and birds when He said:

> Why do you worry about clothing? Consider the lilies of the field, how they grow: they neither toil nor spin; and yet I say to you that even Solomon in all his glory was not arrayed like one of these. Now if God so clothes the grass of the field, which today is, and tomorrow is thrown into the oven, will He not much more clothe you, O you of little faith? Therefore do not worry, saying, "What shall we eat?" or "What shall we drink?" or "What shall we wear?" For after all these things the Gentiles seek. For your heavenly Father knows that you need all these things. But seek first the kingdom of God, and His righteousness, and all these things shall be added to you. Therefore do not worry about tomorrow, for tomorrow will worry about its own things. Sufficient for the day is its own trouble (Matthew 6:28-34 NKJV).

You are not alone; you are not forsaken. Now is a perfect time to put your faith to the test. Learning to lean on Christ may be the most rewarding benefit of this layoff. In fact, it could be one of the most valuable lessons of your life. Don't be afraid to share your need with other believers and friends. Let them help you pray and bear the burden. But above all, learn to trust Christ, knowing that He will never leave you or forsake you.

Believe it or not, there can be some rewarding benefits to temporary unemployment. Rather than looking at the job loss as a total disaster and a negative experience, share with your husband the following potential benefits.

1. *You have time to be together as a couple.* You can rediscover each other all over again. Communication and lovemaking need not be crammed into bedtime but can be extended with more quality time for each other.

2. *You have time to reassess your goals and priorities.* You can prayerfully reconsider and reevaluate your personal goals, your family goals, and your spiritual goals.

3. *You have time to talk to God, to read His Word, and to let your faith expand.* You have a perfect opportunity to learn some valuable lessons of faith and trust.

4. *You have time to spend in ministry and volunteer work.* Hospitals, schools, prisons, church, community programs, youth activities, and senior citizen groups all need qualified help. Now is a perfect time for you to expand your service to other people and to feel the benefits of doing something for others that "lays up treasure in heaven."

5. *You have time to spend with your kids.* You may not have the money to take them on those trips you were planning, but a picnic in the backyard, a game beside the fireplace, a good book read under the apple tree, or a visit to the park or zoo can provide unforgettable memories and deepened bonds of love between you and your children.

6. *You have time to do the fix-it jobs and repairs that have waited for so long.* You may not have the money to do major remodeling, but consider the small repairs and odd jobs

around the house that have waited for that spare time. Also some help with household chores would be appreciated and would free both of you to spend some time together in romance, taking walks together, and communicating.

RESOURCES

Living More with Less. Doris Janzen Longacre. Herald Press, 1980.

QUESTION 31

> ## I feel unorganized and frustrated by life. How can I break this pattern?

You feel overwhelmed, and you ask yourself, "What's the right priority—husband, kids, entertainment, activities, housework, shopping, church activities, Little League, choir rehearsal, or spring cleaning?" The car needs repairs, the lawn needs to be mowed, it's time to do the laundry again, and meals need cooking. To top it all off, maybe you have an outside job too!

And the kids argue. It seems they have to be told things again and again. You find yourself saying, "I'm the only one around here who does anything!"

Does this sound like your house? Do you feel overwhelmed by what's expected of you? If so, you are not alone. Thousands of women feel these feelings of frustration. This is no doubt one of the more frequent requests for help we receive.

Here are some suggestions that can help you get things in order and give control of your life back to you.

1. *Learn to recognize your limitations.* There is only so much that one person can effectively do. All of us need to recognize our limitations. When we stretch ourselves beyond our limitations we become frustrated, depressed, angry, or just burned out.

A. *Learn to delegate.* Delegate some of the household tasks to your husband and children. You say, "It's more work to get my kids to make their beds or pick up their dirty clothes than it is for me to just do it myself." That may be true now because of the habits you have permitted to accumulate in your children. However, it doesn't have to be that way. Each child should have daily and weekly chores that *must* be done. Consequences of not doing them should be consistent and severe enough to matter to the child.

When we are consistent (i.e., every time Johnny forgets to make his bed he is denied the opportunity of playing with his friends that afternoon when he gets home from school), it isn't long until good habits are formed.

Emilie Barnes, a regular columnist in *Virtue* magazine, tells how she delegated chores to her five children and husband in her book *More Hours in My Day.* "Take all of the chores for the week and put them in a basket. Then go around one by one and allow the children to pick out a chore. It was like a little game; whatever they chose were the chores they had to do for the week."

Then she would write them down under each child's name on a daily work-planner chart. Says Emilie, "This relieves you because they don't get mad at you. They've chosen their own chore."

Sit down with your family and make a list of all the chores and let them know that the old system of leaning on Mom is over! From now on everyone pitches in.

B. *Make a daily schedule.* Everyone's chores should be written on a schedule and pinned up somewhere for everyone to refer to. Tape them on the refrigerator or somewhere that can easily be seen. Make a place for checkmarks so that each child can check off a square when his or her task is done. Give them stickers on their chart toward a weekly allowance or other tangible reward.

2. *Learn to control your environment, rather than having your environment control you.* Too often we let life just happen to us rather than controlling and planning our life. Some of us are like a stick floating in the river, being bumped along by rocks, swept up by rapids, then shuttled off into a shallow somewhere or caught on a snag. We feel as if life is surrounding, manipulating, and often drowning us. We feel that

circumstances have robbed us of choice and that we are just victims of what comes our way.

This does not have to be! While some things are unavoidable interruptions to our carefully planned schedules, we can learn to take more control of our environment and the direction of our lives, and what we do with our time.

Here are some suggestions.

A. *Learn the art of saying no.* Susie, the PTA chairman, calls and says, "Hi, we just had our spring fair planning meeting and several people suggested that you were an ideal person to head up the program committee. Will you help us?"

For an instant you want to say no, but guilt floods in since you *do* have two kids in school, and you want to do your share. Reluctantly you say, "Well, okay, I think I can help out."

You hang up the phone, bite your lower lip, silently kick yourself for saying yes, and add this new responsibility to your already-overcrowded schedule.

If this ever happens to you, you are the type of person who needs to discover the art of saying no. Here is how to handle those occasions.

When you feel reluctance or hesitation, tell the person that you will have to check your schedule and call him or her back with an answer tomorrow. This gives you time to think and consider the job. Ask for particulars: dates, planning meeting times, what's involved, etc.

After you have assessed the situation, and if you determine that you really do not have time and that taking on the task would create undue pressure, call Susie back and tell her, "Susie, I have evaluated my schedule for next month and I simply don't have enough time to do a good job. I'm flattered that you asked me to participate. I have marked next year's calendar for spring fair. If you need some help next year, please let me know as far in advance as possible and I'll do my best to schedule the time to do it. But for now I must decline."

Sometimes you know right away that you cannot or should not do something. "Linda is having a Tupperware party next Thursday night—can you come?" You remember that this is the one night you and your husband planned dinner out. "No, I already have an engagement planned for Thursday night. Maybe next time—thank you for the invitation."

Be tough with your schedule. When you already feel swamped, say *no* to additional things that will only frustrate you and make you resent life and put off the other things you should be doing.

B. *Keep a calendar.* This will help you remember where you and everyone else in the family is supposed to be and when they are supposed to be there. It will quickly point out schedule conflicts and will act as an excellent daily, weekly, and monthly reminder. It also gives you power to control much of your time.

Instead of "We never seem to have time to just spend a day together as a family," you can say "Saturday, July 16, is blocked off as family day at the park" or "Monday, two weeks from now, is blocked off for me to go shopping by myself."

At our house we tape a large monthly calendar on the refrigerator door with everyone's activities and appointments, so we can see at a glance what's happening. (We also keep a yearly calendar in another place.)

C. *Make lists!* I'm a believer in making lists. Lists help you organize your life.

My first list is a *things to do* list. This list helps me prioritize my day. After I make a rough list of all the things I need to do and want to do today, I list them in priority: "must do," "should do," "would like to do." You would be amazed at how much more you can get done when you stick to your list!

My next list is a *people* list. People are important to me. I list the people I need to call or write to. These are not business contacts but are people I want to call and encourage, or order some flowers for, or send a card to or drop a note of thanks to. Including a couple of short phone calls, I can get through my *people* list in 30 to 60 minutes. This can become the best 30 minutes of your day—investing in other people, being an encourager.

Other lists include a *grocery list.* Every household should have a list that hangs somewhere in the kitchen. When you reach for the vanilla flavoring and see that it's almost gone, go to the list and jot it down. If you do this with everything, when shopping day comes you won't have to wrack your brain: "What was it I was going to buy?"

You will also need a *maintenance list.* You have decided to refinish Johnnie's chest of drawers. What do you need? Brushes, thinner, masking tape, paint, sandpaper. Check what you already have and be sure to take your list to buy the rest. Nothing is more frustrating than to be all set to do a refinishing project or bake something special and then find out, after everything is spread out ready to go, that you're missing *one thing* needed to complete the project.

Also keep an *important dates list,* for birthdays, anniversaries, special days, etc. This can be put on your calendar or on a separate list. Nothing is more telltale about our organizational skills than belated birthday, anniversary, and Mother's Day cards!

3. *Reprogram yourself.* All these suggestions will work only if you work them. Reprogram yourself to go by your calendars, schedule, and lists.

This doesn't mean that you are unhuman, impersonable, or inflexible. *It means that you are in control.* You are determining what you will do with your time rather than being paralyzed by an overwhelming flood of demands that leaves you wondering where to start.

A schedule actually gives you freedom—freedom for smelling the flowers, for recreation time, for family time. You will be in control, and you will have the great feeling that for the most part circumstances are not controlling you, but you are controlling your circumstances.

RESOURCES

More Hours in My Day. Emilie Barnes. Harvest House Publishers, 1982.

Discipline of Simplicity. Richard Foster. Harper and Row, 1981.

Disciplines of the Beautiful Woman. Anne Ortlund. Word Books, 1977.

Balancing Life's Demands. J. Grant Howard. Multnomah Press, 1983.

QUESTION 32_____

We have a very limited budget. What are some good ways to stretch our dollar?

Many people face tight finances. Some face them because their income is limited. Some people have financial problems because they do not plan their spending. "Tight" finances is a relative term. What is tight to one family may be quite liberal to another.

Regardless of our economic level, many of us find things tight sometimes. While many of the following suggestions are geared to the lower-income bracket, several points are good advice for anyone at any level.

1. *Plan ahead.* Nothing will catch you dollar-short quicker than not planning ahead.

A. *Adopt a budget.* A good plan begins with a budget. A budget is often thought to be a restriction on spending. On the contrary, a budget means freedom to know how to spend, when to spend, and what to buy. A budget takes the anxiety and frustration out of next month. There are several good books on financial planning and budgeting. Take a look at the Resources list at the end of this section for budget guidelines and helps.

B. *Avoid impulse purchases.* These can run from throwing a magazine or pack of gum in your cart while standing at the checkout line to buying a new Corvette during your lunch hour because you couldn't resist the color and good deal.

Whatever your level of impulse buying, unless you have substantial reserves, it will severely impact your budget.

Little things add up quickly. A new record album, an extra ten dollars on Sally's wedding gift, that new fishing rod—all add up to substantial dollars at the end of the month.

I'm not suggesting that you omit all enjoyment from your life, but rather that you budget your recreation, entertainment, and gift money and then stick to your plan.

C. *Plan your meals.* Thursday's specials in the newspaper make a good time to plan next week's menu. When you go to the store, buy what you need, but only what you need. I've noticed many two- to five-year-olds sitting in the infant seats of the grocery shopping carts all across America and begging for junk food! Many people find that it works best to avoid taking the children shopping.

Not only should you plan your meals and stick to your grocery list, but you should try to buy your staples (sugar, flour, soap, etc.) in the most economical sizes. Check the price per pound or per ounce and see which size is the best buy.

Be aware of brand-name psychology. Some brand-name items are better in quality, but with other items it may not be any better, if as good. Often the generic or house brand is packaged by the same company as the higher-priced brand name. You're just paying for their marketing campaigns.

D. *Look for bargains.* Right after Christmas you can get terrific bargains on wrapping paper and greeting cards for next year. Coats go on sale in the spring. Often garage sales have slightly used merchandise at terrific bargains. Read the classified-ad sections of newspapers to find great buys on just about anything.

2. *Avoid credit purchases.* Major items such as a home or car must be purchased on credit. But other credit purchases can become a deadly trap as they eat up a substantial amount of your income in interest. There is no quicker way to wind up in deep financial trouble than through uncontrolled credit buying.

It is far better to save toward a planned purchase and be able to shop for the best deal because you are paying cash.

3. *Learn to tithe.* Some people say they can't afford to give 10 percent of their gross income to God. I believe the opposite is true: We can't afford *not* to tithe.

Tithing is giving back to God His share of what He has given to us. Tithing will not make you richer, but it will put your finances in right standing with God.

Tithing should go on the top of your budget, not on the bottom. It should be your first monthly or weekly payment. If you're not tithing already, try it and you will see that you can make it financially because you will just be giving back to God what rightfully belongs to Him in the first place!

4. *Conserve.* Americans are consumers. Often we consume too much. America comprises 6 percent of the world's population, but we consume 50 percent of the world's goods!

Here are some ways we can conserve.

Plan your week ahead to make one less trip in the car. Leave 20 minutes earlier, slow down 10 miles per hour, and get better gas mileage. Turn off all the lights in rooms not occupied. Wear a sweater and turn down the heat. Wrap your water heater with insulation and put flow restrictors on the showerheads. Call your electric and/or gas company. In most states they will come out free of charge and show you many ways to save on energy.

5. *Be resourceful.* Often there is extra work that you or your family can do to earn extra income. There's a whole new wave of cottage industries (people manufacturing things in their home). You can also do babysitting, sewing, ironing, baking, typing, bookkeeping in your home, etc. Put a small ad in the newspaper.

Plow up some of the lawn in the backyard in a sunny spot and plant a garden. It's great fun as a family project, and all will enjoy watching it grow.

Sew your own clothes, make your own gifts, and have a garage sale for unwanted items or outgrown clothing. There are many alternatives. Put your creativity to work and be resourceful.

6. *Save.* No matter how little you make, try to plan your

budget so that something, however small, can be put away. This will build a reserve for unexpected emergencies, for future major purchases, for your children's college education, for that long-awaited special vacation, or for whatever else may come. *Everyone* should be saving something.

7. *Trust God to meet your needs.* God is interested in your stewardship. He often uses finances to teach us important lessons. Learn to give Him ownership of all you have. You are His and all you have is His. He has entrusted you as a steward. Let Him be the Master, the Owner, and you the servant and faithful steward. When we respond to Him, He will lead us and never fail us.

RESOURCES

Living More with Less. Doris Janzen Longacre. Herald Press, 1981.

You Can Live on Half Your Income. Camilla Dayton Luckey. Zondervan, 1982.

Money in the Cookie Jar. Edith Flowers Kilgo. Baker Book House, 1980.

It Only Hurts Between Paydays. Amy Ross Young. Accent Books.

Part VIII_____

Spiritual Growth

QUESTION 33

> **How can I make my prayer life more effective?**

At times all of us struggle with our prayer life. Distractions, crowded priorities, inconsistencies, discouragement, and many other factors interfere with our prayer life.

Often our prayer life is reduced to bedtime, mealtime, worship services, and occasionally asking God to help us with our problems. While this is prayer in its simplest form, it is not as effective as a disciplined, planned approach to our prayer life.

Here are some keys to developing an effective prayer life.

1. *Learn to offer praise and thanksgiving to God.* Psalm 100:4 says, "Enter into his gates with thanksgiving and into his courts with praise." Praise and thanksgiving set the attitude in your prayer that invites God into the conversation. The Bible indicates that the Lord *inhabits* the praises of His people (Psalm 22:3).

We can practice praising God just about anywhere—doing the dishes, in the car, in our conversations with others, and even in adverse situations.

It is interesting to note that the opposite of praise is blame. There are three categories of persons we blame. First, some of us blame God: "Why me, Lord? Why was I born this way? Why did these circumstances come into my life?" In other words, we attribute all the bad things we go through as an act of God. This not only leads to a false image of God (a sadistic deity taking pleasure in my suffering) but it also leads to bitterness.

Second, and most common, we blame other people. There is an automatic defense mechanism in all of us that seems to immediately trigger when we are cornered or confronted with a serious mistake or problem: We look outward to find the guilty party. The potential weight of admission of guilt or error seems to trigger this defense mechanism.

We have a culprit in our household that always gets the blame. His name is "Not Me!" When Bill's tools are left out to rust in the yard, when the sofa cushions or other debris are left scattered about the family room, when the hot water faucet or light is left on in the bathroom, we as parents go searching for the guilty party. Often the first response is "Not Me!"

As we grow up, we tend to develop one of two personality modes toward other people—either suspicious and critical or else trusting and complimentary. Relating this to good health, someone has said that we are either a nutritious person or a toxic person. A nutritious person is one who conveys goodness, love, and positive feedback to others, while a toxic person is one who brings negativism, criticism, and bitterness. Ask yourself if you are a nutritious or a toxic person. Being a "blamer" can lead you to an attitude of unforgiveness.

Third, we tend to blame ourselves. If there are mistakes we have made, or traits in our personality, or some physical characteristic that we detest, we tend to develop a negative attitude toward ourselves. This leads to feelings of inadequacy and of doubting God's love for us.

If you recognize the trait of blame (toward God, other people, or yourself), you must be willing to forgive and release these attitudes. If you hold on to wrong attitudes of blame, your prayers will be hindered.

2. *Don't always pray with a selfish eye toward what you want.* The book of James, chapter 4, indicates that prayer can actually be self-seeking. James says that many times we do not receive what we pray for because our whole aim is wrong; we pray selfish prayers that are directed at satisfying our own desires.

This is not to say that we should never ask God for things we desire. But our entire prayer life should not be geared to what *I* want for me, but what *God* wants for me. It was Jesus who prayed in the most trying hour of His life, "Nevertheless, not what I will but what You will" (Mark 14:36 NKJV).

3. *Remove known hindrances to prayer.* The first of these hindrances to prayer has already been mentioned, but is worth talking about again: *unforgiveness.* I cannot emphasize enough that there is strong Scriptural evidence that unforgiveness will not allow your prayers to be effective. Jesus said in Matthew 5:23,24:

> Therefore if you bring your gift to the altar, and there remember that your brother has something against you, leave your gift there before the altar, and go your way. First be reconciled to your brother, and then come and offer your gift (NKJV).

In Matthew 6:14,15 Jesus also said:

> For if you forgive men their trespasses, your heavenly Father will also forgive you. But if you forgive not men their trespasses, neither will your Father forgive your trespasses.

The second hindrance to prayer is *common distractions.* Here are several usual ones and how to handle them.

A. *The telephone.* This has a simple solution: *Take it off the hook!* The telephone has incredible power in our lives. In most businesses or homes, even in the middle of serious business or important conversation, if the phone rings, *everything* must stop so someone can answer the phone. If someone in person interrupted us like that, we would consider it very rude. If you really want to talk to God, don't let the phone interrupt your time.

B. *Busy thoughts.* I found myself thinking about all the things I had to do while praying. I also found that some of my most creative ideas came while praying. So I decided to take a pencil and paper with me to prayer. Now I can write down the things I need to do and forget about them because I've committed them to paper. I can also get my creative inspirations and blueprints down and then go on with my prayers.

C. *Kids/others need me.* Plan your prayer time when you are alone—when the kids are at school, your husband is at work, the baby is sleeping, or when someone else is there to tend to their needs. You could even hire a babysitter for an hour or so. After all, we hire babysitters for everything else, so why not for prayer time? If you cannot afford one, maybe you could trade babysitting prayer time with another Christian neighbor or friend.

D. *Wandering mind.* Make a prayer list to keep your mind from wandering and to give specific substance to your prayer. First, write down a list of specific things for which you wish to thank and praise God. Include not only thanks for the things He has done, but also for who He is. Next, list the people and situations that need prayer. Be specific so that you can pray intelligently. God does not object to organized prayer. David the psalmist organized entire days for prayer and praise. He planned festive occasions with dancers, musicians, and an entire nation offering up prayer to God.

4. *Maintain a regular devotional life.* This takes both habit and discipline. Prayer is not only to be offered when we *feel* like it, but is most effective when consistent, whether we feel like it or not. You can be honest with God. It's okay to say, "God, I really don't feel like praying today, but I'm here because I love you and I know You are there."

Get used to these two emotions when it comes to your prayer life: First, you will not always *feel* like praying; second, it is not always a joyous, refreshing experience.

At times you will feel that your prayers go no further than the ceiling. At other times your prayer life will be a wonderfully refreshing and enlightening experience. Form a habit, be consistent, and don't go by how you feel!

5. *Learn to wait and listen.* Too often we rush into the

presence of God and go through our list of things to pray for and then rush out to rejoin the rest of life without ever waiting to hear from God. I have a mental picture of God patiently waiting His turn while we pour out our hearts to Him. Then, just about the time He can get a word in, we leave His presence, never waiting for a response. Isaiah 40:31 says, "But they that *wait* upon the Lord shall renew their strength; they shall mount up with wings as eagles, they shall run and not be weary; they shall walk and not faint."

6. *Pray together as well as alone.* Nothing can replace your personal private prayer time with God. But try to include others, especially your family, in times of prayer. When you pray with your children, you are actually teaching them how to pray and teaching them lessons of faith and trust in God. How can we expect our kids to learn effective prayer unless we teach them how to pray and for what to pray? When you share real needs with your children, and then they see God supply an answer to prayer, it is a wonderful faith-builder in showing them that prayer is effective.

Some surveys indicate that there are a very small percentage of Christian couples who regularly pray together. You can be the exception! Here are some simple guidelines regarding prayer with your husband, especially if he is currently failing to take the initiative.

A. *Don't insist that he initiate it.* I know about spiritual headship and leadership, but it is better to have wife-initiated prayer than no prayer. Eventually, when it becomes an enjoyable habit in your relationship, he will initiate it.

B. *Keep it brief.* Even a minute or two of agreeing in prayer together in the beginning is better than no prayer. As you both warm up to the idea and feel comfortable, let your prayer time develop into a longer time together.

C. *Pray conversationally.* Talk to God as you would talk to each other. Both of you add a sentence or two about a need or subject. Be natural and pray about everyday needs and problems, such as work, kids, health, finances, etc. Also, thank God for everyday provisions.

D. *Don't preach in prayer.* A couple's prayer time together will be destroyed if it is used to nag or to point out a spouse's faults: "O Lord, You know how bad Jerry needs to quit overeating," or "I know, Lord, that You are repulsed by Fred's attitude and behavior toward me," or "Show Dick that this situation is not Your will, Lord." This type of prayer is sure to turn your spouse off to prayer and make him extremely reluctant to want to pray with you the next time.

E. *Always clear the air before you pray.* First Peter 3:7 indicates that our prayers will be hindered if there is not mutual love, forgiveness, respect, and honor toward each other before entering into prayer.

Finally, pray in the name of Jesus because He is our Advocate with the Father. As our Savior, He becomes our Mediator toward God the Father. Have faith that God will answer your prayers. They may not always be the answers you expect, but God does answer prayer. "The effective, fervent prayer of a righteous man avails much" (James 5:16 NKJV).

RESOURCES

Practicing the Presence of God. A.W. Tozer. Christian Publications, 1948.

How to Keep a Spiritual Journal. Ronald Klug. Thomas Nelson Publishers, 1982.

A Life of Prayer. St. Teresa of Avila. Abridged edition by Multnomah Press, 1983.

Answers to Prayer. Charles G. Finney. Compiled by Louis Gifford Parkhurts, Jr., Bethany Fellowship, 1983.

QUESTION 34

> ## How do I learn to enjoy Bible study on my own?

You are not alone if you are a person who struggles with finding time to spend in God's Word or lack the enjoyment you wished you had in reading the Bible. Bible reading and study must be placed as a priority in our life in the day and culture in which we live.

Certainly there are enough hours in the day. Often we use the excuse that we simply don't have the time. Working, sleeping, socializing, and family time are all a part of each 24 hours. If we schedule our lives properly in right priority, we will find the time to enjoy God's Word. Dr. James Braga's book *How to Study the Bible* offers some suggestions that I think will help.

1. *Be consistent.* Establish a priority time that is yours alone to read God's Word. Behaviorists tell us that it takes about 21 days to form a new habit. Work on your schedule, and find a time that's good for you. It should be a relaxed time (at least 30 minutes) when you will be relatively free from interruptions—maybe when the kids are off to school, or your little one is having his afternoon nap, or at night after everyone is tucked in. Find a quiet place, disconnect the phone, and say, "God, this is our time together in Your Word." Above all, do it regularly.

2. *Be systematic.* Study God's Word with a plan. Don't just close your eyes and open the Bible, hoping that a passage will pop out at you. Instead, pick a certain book, start with chapter 1, and continue daily until the book is finished.

There are dozens of daily Bible study helps that can assist you in a systematic approach.

3. *Read the Bible.* This may sound strange to say, but many people read books *about* the Bible or listen to taped sermons and talks, but seldom read the Bible for themselves. These other helps are wonderful, but they can never substitute for the Word of God itself. God can speak to you and give you fresh insights when you read and meditate on His Word, rather than always having it predigested for you.

Don't begin a Bible study program with commentaries, tapes, and other people's ideas. These can be excellent helps to shed light on Scripture, but if these are the first exposure we have to a passage, we can then only see the passage through the commentator's eyes, rather than seeing the fresh insight that the Holy Spirit may want to bring to us.

4. *Read meditatively.* Psalm 1:1,2 states, "Blessed is the man that walketh not in the counsel of the ungodly, nor standeth in the way of sinners, nor sitteth in the seat of the scornful. But his *delight* is in the law of the Lord, and in his law doth he *meditate* day and night."

To meditate and delight simply means to think...ponder...wait...discover...reread...think...ponder...wait...discover.

You can discover wonderful gems of truth and insight if you learn to meditate on the Word of God!

5. *Use your imagination and creativity.* When you are reading a narrative, place yourself into the study by imagining what the scenery and clothing were like, what the weather and mood were, etc. All of us have been given creative imaginations and can visualize settings. This will help you to retain the passage and its implications.

As an example, read Esther 1:1-8. Notice the description of this incredible celebration in the Shushan palace. Imagine the lavish decorations detailed in verse 6. Think of the dignitaries invited, all their pomp and dress, the golden goblets of royal wine, etc.

Think about the people, the places, the houses, the

objects, what might have been said by observers, etc.

6. *Learn in context.* Be sure to study Scripture within its context. Learn to read the chapter preceding and the chapter following. Scripture quoted out of context can be misleading to both you and other people.

7. *Pray for guidance.* Ask God, by His Holy Spirit, to illumine the Scriptures to you and to give you His insight and understanding. It is when the Scriptures begin to speak to us *personally* that Bible study becomes a source of blessing, joy, and personal enrichment.

8. *Be quick to respond and obey.* The study of Scripture will inevitably produce insights into our own life and patterns of behavior. When truth is revealed to us through God's Word, we must be quick to act on that truth in obedience to God's will. This will sharpen our sensitivity to God and His will and make us even more perceptive in our Bible study.

Personal Bible study is a great adventure holding inexhaustible riches for you to discover. Get going now and you'll find a lifetime of treasure awaiting you!

RESOURCES

Getting More from Your Bible. Terry Hall. Victor Books, 1984.
What the Bible Is All About. Henrietta Mears. Regal Books, 1953.
12 Dynamic Bible Study Methods. Richard Warren. Victor Books, 1978.
How to Study the Bible. James Braga. Multnomah Press.

QUESTION 35

How do I accept Jesus Christ as my Savior and Lord?

Without question, the most wonderful thing that God has ever done for the human race is to give us the gift of salvation. By understanding and accepting Jesus Christ, God's Son, we can be reconciled to God, receive forgiveness for sin, and inherit eternal life.

Everyone who comes to this point of decision has his or her own set of unique circumstances that brought him or her to this point. But the one thing that is the same for all of us is the admission that we are sinners in need of a Savior, asking Christ to come into our lives, and at that moment receiving forgiveness and a new life in Christ.

The Bible, God's Word, tells us, "All have sinned, and come short of the glory of God" (Romans 3:23). This means that all of us are in need of a Savior. John 3:16 says, "God so loved the world that he gave his only begotten Son, that whoever believes in him should not perish, but have everlasting life."

It is important for us to realize that salvation is a free gift from God, and that there is nothing we can do to earn or deserve this wonderful gift. In Ephesians 2:8,9 we read, "For by grace you have been saved, through faith, and that not of yourselves; it is the gift of God—not of works, lest anyone should boast" (NKJV).

This means that all our own efforts at self-improvement in order to gain God's favor are fruitless. Notice the words in the passage above: "grace," "faith," and "gift." *Grace* means "unmerited favor." We can do nothing to deserve God's favor. *Faith* means "trust in God." What God says to us in His Holy Word is true: He will keep His promise to save us if we ask Him to do so. *Gift* means that God's grace or unmerited favor in saving us is *free*: There is nothing we can do to buy or earn it.

Often people give reasons why they feel they must try to "earn" God's favor, approval, and forgiveness. Here are some common reasons.

1. I've always had to earn other people's approval.
2. Society tells us that good people go to heaven and bad people to go hell.
3. I feel guilt over habitual sin.
4. I'm such a bad person; why would God want me?
5. I'm not such a bad person; why would God send me to hell?
6. God helps those who help themselves.
7. As soon as I get this problem in my life straightened out, I'll come to God.
8. Crying out to God when you have a problem is a cop-out and a sign of weakness.

It's interesting to note that all of these excuses involve guilt, pride, and works rather than *grace*, *faith*, and *gift!*

In order to have forgiveness from sin and freedom from death, and to experience God's grace and redemption, we must cast ourselves openly and humbly on God's mercy. In 1 John 1:9 we read, "If we confess our sins, he is faithful and just to forgive us our sins, and to cleanse us from all unrighteousness."

Now is a good time for you to ask Christ to help you. Confess your sin to Him and ask Him to come into your life. Here's one prayer that you can pray:

Lord Jesus, I am a sinner. I confess my sins to You, asking You to forgive me. I believe that You died on the cross for my sin. I believe that You are alive again today and that by Your death and resurrection You have the power to forgive my sin and put me in right standing with God. Come into my heart and begin to make my life new. Show me how to be Your follower, and teach me Your way of living. Thank You for Your gift of salvation. Amen.

This is a simple prayer, but this is all it takes to become God's child, because God has done everything else for you. Here are some Scripture passages for you to read:

- The Gospel of John
- Ephesians chapter 2
- Romans chapter 8

If you don't attend church already, find a good church. Ask God to help you find one that teaches the Bible every week in terms you can understand. The church denomination is not the important issue, but whether or not they actually teach the Bible. When picking a church, ask the pastor, "Is this an evangelical church that teaches the Bible?" If he says no, or hesitates, then continue to look for a church where the pastor enthusiastically says yes. You will be happy in this type of church and will begin to grow in your walk with the Lord.

It is also *extremely important* for you to spend personal, consistent time reading God's Word and talking with God in prayer. See the preceding chapters.

QUESTION 36

> **My husband is not a believer. What's the best way to bring him to Christ?**

It is not uncommon today for a Christian woman to find herself "unequally yoked" with an unbelieving husband. She may have married her husband with the idea, "I can win him to the Lord after we're married." Or she may have thought her husband was a believer before marriage, only to discover later that her husband never really made a commitment to Christ. Or she may have found Christ since marriage and would now like to see her husband share the joy of her salvation too.

In today's American society, most men have a hard time admitting that they are in need of help and humbling themselves to ask for forgiveness and cleansing. And the "macho" image makes it especially hard for a man to "follow" his wife into a commitment.

Dr. Theodore Rubin, columnist for *Ladies Home Journal*, says American men in general:

- Don't like to admit they are dependent.
- Are fearful, jealous, and contemptuous of women.
- Will not admit soft, warm feelings, which they consider feminine.
- Feel they must be strong (i.e. stubborn, competitive).
- Are unable to measure up to masculine ideals.
- Won't admit it, but they crave affection.
- Are frightened by the possibility of rejection by women.
- Measure self-esteem in terms of power and money.

While all of these characteristics may not be shown by your unbelieving husband, some of them could be motivating factors in any hesitancy he may have in accepting your faith.

I should add that even *after* your husband comes to Christ, some of these characteristics, as well as other negative behavior, will still be evident. Be careful not to set your expectations too high. Your husband is human and will need lots of time and room to grow.

The remainder of this chapter deals with some actions to avoid and some actions to take, quoted from Jerry Mason's article, "Moving Your Man Toward the Light," in the March/April 1984 issue of *Virtue* magazine:

Knowing mistakes to avoid is often a key to reaching your man. There are no ironclad rules, but in general a man's identity is inextricably bound to his ego and pride. If either are gored, he can become like an enraged bull, intent on attacking the one who wounded him. Problems with self-esteem can become major obstacles if not handled sensitively. The following tips can help.

1. *Don't use force.* God doesn't violate anyone's freedom of choice. Yet some women try forceful tactics, such as threatening to withdraw affection if their man doesn't believe as they do. Should the "cold shoulder" approach succeed in pressuring him into a relationship with Christ, it would be for the wrong reason. He would be making a decision just to please someone else, not because of his desire to follow the Lord. Every person should seek God on his own initiative, not because he "had to" to appease another person. I came to the Living Water because of the positive effects I saw it had on my wife, Linda. I wasn't forced to drink. I was thirsty, and I came willingly.

2. *Don't be impatient.* Steel doesn't bend unless exposed to extreme heat. Since "macho men" are supposed to be as strong as steel, change for them is difficult. Don't expect too much too soon. Unrealistic expectations generally lead to unnecessary problems.

Start by accepting and loving your man the way the Lord does—just as he is.

A mountain can be moved either by a miracle, an earthquake, or lots of time, energy, and earth-moving equipment. I was a nonbeliever for two-thirds of my life. I'm thankful that the Lord and Linda devoted years of patient effort to help reshape the hardened parts, and to help me become the man God wants me to be. Take it one step at a time and try not to become frustrated if everything doesn't go just as you planned. Persistence, patience, faith, and love are some of your best mountain-moving tools.

3. *Don't compromise your faith.* A "macho" man values integrity in people. Even if he may not agree with all that they stand for, he will usually respect them if their actions are consistent with their beliefs. Undoubtedly your man has encountered what he believes to be "hypocritical Christians." Check yourself. Are you faithful to what you profess? Do you regularly read and apply God's Word to your life? Do you consistently pray and communicate with Him? Does he see the Lord reflected in your life and in your attitude toward those in the home?

Stand firm in your convictions, even if he tests you to see if you really believe what you say. I tested Linda often, and it wore on her. Yet I respected her for not giving in to the pressures I applied. If he challenges you, respond in love. The tenor of your response will speak louder than your words. If he tries to involve you in something that compromises your beliefs, briefly explain your position without putting him down and suggest an alternative that you both can enjoy.

4. *Don't badger or be argumentative.* Proverbs 27:15 says that a quarrelsome wife is like a constant dripping on a rainy day. In other words, she can be a real irritant to her man. Knowing that a woman's behavior is a powerful force in influencing her husband, Peter wrote, "If they refuse to listen when you talk to them about the Lord, they will be won by your respectful, pure behavior. Your godly lives will

speak to them better than any words" (1 Peter 3:2 TLB). A man will probably respond better to a warm, peaceful "light" than to a thundering bolt striking out with verbal abuse.

Now that you're aware of some of the pitfalls to avoid, let your light shine brightly before the man you love. Here are some actions to take.

1. *Live out your faith.* Men are strongly influenced by what they observe in the lives of others. Jesus knew that men would be skeptical. That's why He came to earth and became Emmanuel, God with us. It was His example on earth that won men to Himself.

If your man sees faith in God working in your life and in the lives of other Christians whom he respects, he will be affected positively. If, on the other hand, he observes that knowing God doesn't seem to make a difference, forget it. He needs to witness your faith at work in the everyday nitty-gritty of life.

2. *Be kind and loving, even if it isn't reciprocated.* As Dr. Rubin said, "Men crave affection but won't admit it."

Love allures and compels men. And it draws even more powerfully if it's given freely and unconditionally in the midst of trying circumstances. The in-spite-of, Christlike love for your man comes not from you alone, but from the One who is Love Himself. Allow Him to love through you.

3. *Appeal to reason, but don't forget his emotional side.* Your man probably respects the intellect because he's learned to live by his own wits. Consequently, a well-reasoned, intellectual defense of your faith can be powerful.

Many people cannot adequately explain what (or why) they believe. If you are unable to give a sound "reason for the hope that is in you" (1 Peter 3:15), work on it. Read, study, question, think, ask, and pray.

Realize that a man's emotions and his will are major driving forces behind the decisions he makes. So, while trying to influence his mind, never underestimate the power of an appeal to his heart. Men are much more driven by emotion than they usually admit.

4. *Don't expect perfection.* Men are somewhat like trees: They can bend easily when they're supple seedlings, but not when they're mature, forest monarchs. It's very difficult to get adult men to grow in radically different directions. If you enter into a relationship expecting to transform an oak into a willow, it probably won't happen. "Accept me as I am and I can change," is a powerful concept. Demanding perfection will result in discouragement and frustration. Unconditional acceptance will draw your man more naturally to the Lord.

5. *Get help if you can.* Moving a mountain is discouraging if you're the only one with a shovel. Many men will not or cannot be moved by a lone individual, particularly a woman. In my life, I sought out other men whom I respected and in whom I could confide to help me as I struggled to find answers to my questions. Your man probably needs to do the same. Is there a Christian male with whom he could talk and feel comfortable? If you don't know a flesh-and-blood male, a carefully selected book may help, but don't bury your man with materials if he isn't willing to read them. Encourage him to seek opinions of other male believers. Once he sees that he need not commit intellectual suicide or sacrifice his masculinity to become a Christian, some of his fears may be diminished.

6. *Pray, trust God, and wait.* Be assured that God loves your man more than you do. And, although God will not violate his free will, He is drawing him now if only he will open his eyes and respond.

Looking back, I see that prayer had more effect on me than anything else. Persevering in prayer and trusting God with the outcome will bring more spiritual power to bear on your man than anything you can muster on your own.

Receiving Christ as Savior is ultimately a decision that each individual must make on his own. You can shine a light on the path, but every person must walk it for themselves.

You ask, "But what if I've done everything I can think

of and still he won't move?" Don't give up and don't stop giving him your love and steadfast devotion. Also remember that God knows how you feel. Ask Him to increase His love within you for your unmoving man. (It's possible, too, that God is using him as a tool in your life to refine your character through adversity.)

A hopeful note has been sounded by social trend observer John Naisbett (author of the bestseller *Megatrends*). He has reported that there is a strong movement in America away from the "macho" male role. Men are learning new, more human and open roles which relate more naturally and less stiffly with women.

In the meantime, understanding how your man feels is a key to moving him toward the Light. It may take extra love and patience on your part to relate and to help in trying situations, but the benefits are eternal. Reach out to the man you love and let him see the reflection of Christ's light in your life.

QUESTION 37

> ## How can I encourage my husband to be a stronger spiritual leader in our home?

The Scriptural pattern is for men to be the head of their homes. Ephesians 5:22-25 says, "Wives, submit yourselves unto your own husbands as unto the Lord. For the husband is the head of the wife, even as Christ is the head of the church; and he is the Savior of the body. Therefore as the church is subject unto Christ, so let the wives be to their own husbands in everything. Husbands, love your wives, even as Christ also loved the church and gave himself for it."

There is obviously a two-way street here: *Husband,* love your wife as Christ loved the church; *wife,* respect your husband's leadership.

But many Christian wives are frustrated by what seems to be a lack of spiritual leadership from their husbands in their families. The husband may be reluctant to attend church more than once a week, fail to initiate family devotions, fail to pray with his wife, or fail to read the Bible. This is not an isolated problem relegated only to weak Christians; I have heard this complaint from pastors' and deacons' wives as well. A minister's wife may say, "He ministers to everyone but me and the kids!" These men may be active at church but still not exercising spiritual leadership at home.

There are certain areas in which you can encourage your husband's leadership, and certain areas that you need to leave alone. Some women feel inferior about their abilities and talents, and decide that they must live life vicariously through their husbands—deriving fulfillment from his job, his prestige in the community, his ministry, and perhaps even his spirituality. Although the man is definitely to be the head of his home, all of us must ultimately answer to God *individually*. So while our husband's spirituality may be of great concern to us, it is *not* ultimately our responsibility as wives! Over and over the Bible says, "God is no respecter of persons." We stand before God individually. As wives, we are called to love and respect our husbands— not to play "Holy Spirit" on his behalf.

I realize the anguish there can be in a wife's heart when the husband is not taking his rightful place as the leader. Perhaps the wife has stepped in and taken that job over. Perhaps the husband is walking in disobedience to the Lord. Perhaps he is spiritually immature—or just lazy. Meanwhile, there are the children to consider.

I heard one wife say, "I got so *tired* of pushing! If we were ever to get to church, it was at my initiative. *I* woke everybody up, *I* urged us out the door. If we ever had family devotions, who started it? Me! I'm tired of pushing, and I finally decided that if that's all he cares about the spiritual welfare of our family, I'm through." At last report that family was still out of church.

There are two extremes to avoid: 1) pushing and nagging, and 2) giving up. These are direct reactions to your husband. It is harder to take the "middle road," but in the long run it's the most effective. You will need patience, wisdom, and prayer. Galatians 6:9 says, "Let us not be weary in well-doing, for in due season we shall reap, if we faint not."

First, examine your own motives for your frustrations for your husband's spiritual role. Are you dissatisfied with your own spiritual condition? Are you comparing your husband to someone else's spouse and finding your husband lacking? Things are not always as they appear! That man in your church who seems to be the ideal spiritual leader may be unbearable to live with at home. First Peter 3:1 says, "Be subject to your *own* husband."

Try to understand where your husband is coming from.

Often men have been schooled to be "macho" and to suppress their emotions. Women are freer to express their feelings. A woman may have more opportunities than her husband to grow spiritually: She may have access to women's meetings, Bible studies, etc. A wife's spiritual "prowess" can be intimidating to her husband. He may subconsciously feel, "Well, she's obviously more spiritual than I am, so she can just take over that department of the family." Your husband may have been raised in a home where his mother was the spiritual leader, and he may feel that this is just the way it is. You may have to subtly retrain him!

Although you cannot force your husband's relationship to God or to his family, you *can*—

- pray for him
- love him
- encourage him
- edify him
- relinquish your "hold" on him by giving him to God.

These are powerful tools! Don't feel ill-equipped or locked into a pattern for life.

Prayer is a key ingredient. Through prayer for your husband and your family, God will give you wisdom and direction. "Pray without ceasing" (1 Thessalonians 5:17).

Love is something that you show or do—not sermonettes! It's the little things that mean so much—his favorite food, expressions of love and appreciation. Before you get your husband's ear, you must win his heart.

Encourage him in his spiritual leadership at home. When you sit down to a meal, defer to him. Let him ask the blessing, or let him ask someone to ask the blessing. Look at him and wait for him. If he looks back at you with a blank look, you can say, "Did you want me to ask the blessing, Dear?" If he says yes, then *he* has made a decision! It may be a tiny one at first, but encourage him. Ask him whether, if you schedule the time, he would read a portion of Scripture at family devotions. Then get the kids up early enough, or whatever you need to do to set the stage. If he doesn't care to read, you could ask him, "Did you want me to read today?" or "Who would you like to read today?" thus encouraging his active leadership in front of the children.

Edify him by encouraging fellowship or activities with other families and couples in which you feel the man is strong spiritually. It will help your husband to see role models of godly men. If you can, entertain pastors or visiting missionaries in your home. Make a date with another couple to go out to dinner and talk about the things of God in a relaxed, friendly setting. Encourage your husband to attend prayer breakfasts or men's meetings where "real men" are spiritual leaders.

Relinquish him to God—he is in God's hands. God loves him and is working in your husband's life. Meanwhile, *you* be obedient to what the Lord is calling you to do and be. If your husband is a spasmodic church attender, or it's way down on his list of priorities, but he doesn't mind if *you* go to church—do what you know to be right. Take your kids to church with you. When you're tempted to give up, think: "What example, what attitude of mine will make a lasting difference upon this family toward church and the things of God?" If it is a grim determination, a power struggle, church can take on negative connotations. If it is a joyful, willing spirit that is calling you to worship at God's house, this kind of attitude is contagious. You may find yourself getting dressed to go to church and suddenly everyone is wanting to go with you.

Remember, spiritual leadership has a lot more to do with life than who gets the kids up for church. It involves daily attitudes and examples in the home that require a team effort. Daily living of one's Christian virtues in front of your children will do far more for them than a thousand sermons. In today's society, team leadership (both husband and wife cooperating as living examples of God's grace) is by far the most rewarding and effective form of spiritual leadership.

RESOURCES

Maximized Manhood. Edwin L. Cole. Whitaker House, 1982.

Part IX _____

Life Changes

QUESTION 38

> ## Could I be suffering a midlife crisis?

A "midlife crisis" has been commonly thought of as happening to men. Women, we're told, go through the "change of life" (menopause). Recent research, however, indicates that while it usually happens at a younger age for women—35 to 39 (the common age for a man is in the early forties)—there is strong evidence that many women do suffer a midlife crisis.

Symptoms seem to vary, and the advice on how to cope is general, but there is beginning to be a new appreciation and awareness that a crisis does happen in the late thirties for many women.

Jim and Sally Conway in their book *Women In Mid-Life Crisis* call this episode a "collision of expectations and reality." They go on to point out that "a woman is now forced to realize that some of her expectations are never going to be met. For example, she can put up with a poor marriage for years thinking that 'someday soon' it will change, or she may keep hoping to see some of her other personal dreams come true. By mid-life she is faced with the reality that not all of her dreams will be realized."

Midlife crisis is not so much dated by age as it is by stage—that is, where you are in your life cycle. Conway believes that "the bulk of them fall in the mid to late thirties." Says Conway, "Gail Sheehy points out the significance of age 35 as it relates to what we are calling midlife crisis. She lists the following facts of female life that all come to focus at about age 35:

- 34 is when the average mother sends her last child to school
- 35 begins the dangerous age of infidelity
- 35 is when the average married American woman reenters the working world
- 34 is the average age at which the divorced woman takes a new husband
- 35 is the most common age of the runaway wife
- 35 brings the biological boundary into sight."

Midlife can be difficult for all women. Whether divorced, never married, married, career women, homemakers, with or without children, women from all socioeconomic strata and all regions of the country can suffer a midlife crisis.

The Conways state that some or all of the following factors may produce stress or cause a crisis for women:

1. Our present-day cultural view of women
2. An unhappy marriage or lack of marriage
3. Her husband's own midlife crisis
4. Demands from children and their growing independence
5. Career priorities related to other life priorities
6. An accumulation of traumatic losses such as death, illness, or aging
7. Urgency from her inner clock to accomplish her life dreams
8. Imperative reevaluation time to review the past and plan for the future.

It is also at about this time that women start noticing sagging skin, drooping breasts, and flecks of gray hair. When looking in the mirror, some recognize age and perceive a loss of attractiveness. My wife, Nancie, wrote in her journal one day when she was 35, "I get terrified of my own mortality sometimes. It hits me when I cleanse my face and cream it at night, and I see the wrinkles or study the gray hairs in my hair. Even my menstrual cycle fascinates me in a way. I wonder how many more years my body will be fit for childbearing. It's not that I want more children; it's just the *idea*. Or the waistline that seems larger than it was. I know it's *time*, just the process. Why fight it? Why panic over externals? Why grope for the right hairdo, the right makeup to hide the dark circles? I've got to shift the effort, the polishing, to the eternal: fruit of the Spirit, doing God's work in God's way, instilling values in my children. Trying to stop aging is like trying to hold back the sea."

A woman at this stage is also in the process of questioning the value of life. Instead of questioning what she is doing, she begins to ask herself why she is doing it. She feels somewhat worthless in her contribution. She prepares meals, washes clothes, cleans the house, entertains guests, taxis kids, and fulfills her husband's needs, all the while maintaining an amazing stability, a cheerful attitude, and an even temper. But for what? Frequently she feels unappreciated, unnoticed, unattractive, and unnecessary.

After she works in a job for less pay than her male peers, making her boss look good by virtually running the company for him behind the scenes, she feels the same lack of appreciation at work.

It is small wonder that many women begin to resent their role and start thinking of self-actualization and self-fulfillment at this stage of life.

In the book *Stress/Unstress*, Keith W. Sienert, M.D., lists symptoms that may be evident in a woman on the brink of crisis:

- Decision-making becomes difficult (both major and minor kinds)
- Extreme daydreaming and fantasizing about "getting away from it all"
- Increased use of cigarettes and/or alcohol
- Thoughts trail off while speaking or writing
- Excessive worrying about all things
- Sudden outbursts of temper and hostility

- Paranoid ideas and mistrust of friends and family
- Forgetfulness for appointments, deadlines, dates
- Frequent spells of brooding and feelings of inadequacy
- Reversals in usual behavior.

To Sienert's list I would add:

- Compulsive overeating
- Frequent crying spells for no apparent reason
- An affair or strong new fantasies about an affair
- Extreme preoccupation with soap operas and romance novels.

Here are some suggested ways to help you survive a midlife crisis.

1. *Understand what is taking place and hang on to your value system.* You cannot avoid the fact that you are feeling this way and are facing reevaluation of your life. Face it head-on and be willing to reassess and redefine your life goals.

It can be constructive if you will look carefully at your goals and priorities (who I am, where I am going, what I want to accomplish before I die, whom I love, who needs my love, etc.). Says Conway, "Some of your priorities may be the same as before, but some will be discarded and new ones added. Mid-life is one of the times when a great many events force a re-assessment of life." If in all of this you can put deeper trust in God and His Word, if you can stay rooted in His plan and value system, you will ultimately profit from the crisis experience.

2. *Order your life to fit your value system.* Says Conway, "You will experience an emotional crisis if the choices you make and the activities you live out are not in line with your inner value system—that is, your life characteristics, wishes, needs, goals, feelings, your *real self.*"

3. *Spend time in prayer and reading God's Word.* Nothing can strengthen and solidify who you are and where you want to go more than an intimate relationship with Jesus Christ.

The Holy Spirit becomes our Teacher and Guide. Even though we may be confronted and/or disoriented for a time, if we put our trust in Him, He *will* be our Guide.

4. *Share your feelings with a loved one, Christian friend, or counselor.* Having someone to listen and then give a healthy response when we are going through reevaluation is extremely important. Often our trusted friend can have more objectivity than we do during the time of crisis. It also gives us a chance to vent our feelings and thoughts without acting them out. This could help us avoid serious mistakes that we would later regret.

5. *Listen to others.* Often we have our ideas formulated and our minds made up *before* we seek counsel. When we do this, we are not seeking objective counsel, but only someone to agree with our conclusions.

Avoid this trap by seriously considering the feedback you are receiving from others—your Bible, your pastor, your friends, your husband, your family, your counselor, and your conscience. Here are some Scriptures that show God's interest in helping you through any and all crises:

> I will instruct you and teach you in the way you should go; I will guide you with My eye (Psalm 32:8 NKJV).
> Call upon Me in the day of trouble; I will deliver you, and you shall glorify Me (Psalm 50:15 NKJV).
> The Lord will guide you continually, and satisfy your soul in drought, and strengthen your bones; you shall be like a watered garden, and like a spring of water, whose waters do not fail (Isaiah 58:11 NKJV).

RESOURCES

Women in Mid-Life Crisis. Jim and Sally Conway. Tyndale, 1983.
Changepoints. Joyce Landorf. Fleming H. Revell, 1981.
A Woman's Quest for Serenity. Gigi Tchividjian. Fleming H. Revell, 1981.

QUESTION 39

My children are all out of the nest. Where to from here?

We recently counseled a woman whose last child had left for college six months prior to our session. "John is gone off to college, Diane is married and lives in Tacoma, and Danny's been transferred to Denver. We have this big rambling house that seems so empty. I just feel like my life is empty too."

When children leave to establish their own lives, parents (especially mothers) who have given themselves to the raising of their children feel that their purpose in life is over.

H. Norman Wright in an article titled "The Season of the Empty Nest," published in the May/June 1983 issue of *Virtue* magazine, states: "Many studies show that when the last child grows up and leaves home there is an increased likelihood of marital maladjustment. This event acts as a marital catalyst, demanding that the husband and wife face themselves, each other, and their marriage in a new way. The longer they avoid this task, the faster the gap between them widens.

"For one thing, the couple must make adjustments in their parental and spousal roles. This can be especially true for the mother who has devoted herself almost entirely to her children. When they leave she feels abandoned, unloved, and uncared for. When her children grow up, the mother literally joins the ranks of the unemployed. She may begin to feel that there is little reason or justification for her life, that she has little to contribute to the process of living."

Some couples dream of the day when their kids will be gone. They look forward with anticipation to the time when travel and leisure can be enjoyed without the responsibility of children. But the "second honeymoon" does not materialize for everyone. Some women were going to take up writing or find a job or learn to play tennis, only to discover that these activities do not carry with them the meaning and purpose for which they had hoped.

Still others are more optimistic and keep forging through their emotions and adjustments until purpose is regained and some new goals are set.

Dr. Wright gives some important elements in *adjusting* to the empty nest.

1. Learn to develop a new kind of intimacy with each other as you adjust. Learn a new depth of communication that will help both of you adjust and become more intimate friends.

2. Develop a new way of performing your roles. Learn how to share household tasks and to play, plan, and work together.

3. Expand your range of friendships, finding other couples who are in the same situation. By this you can redirect some of the emotional investment once spent on your children to these other friends.

4. Redefine your role with your children. Let the parent-child role mature into an adult-adult role. This is accomplished by avoiding interference with your children's lives and not pushing your advice on them.

5. Give of yourselves in service to others. This is a healthy way to channel our talents and energies and, for Christians, it is a fulfillment of our purpose in life.

Wright goes on to give some specific suggestions in *preparing* for the empty-nest phase of life.

1. Establish your marriage at the top of your priorities. Do this early in life. Often couples are fearful that marriage will interfere with their careers or chances of success, but remember that a lasting marriage, while requiring

commitment, is the best onset for happiness and fulfillment that a person can possess.

2. The demand of parenting should be balanced with the needs of your marriage. Time alone together, daily intimate moments, the care and cultivation of friendship and romance, must be *planned*. This *must* be jealously preserved between you and your spouse.

3. Don't let marriage problems go. Any breakdown in communication, drifting apart, or staleness must be confronted. Ignoring these symptoms leads to indifference.

4. Encourage each other to develop your own spiritual gifts. You cannot be all things to each other. Give each other freedom to be unique. A dominating relationship leads one spouse to feel trapped.

5. Maintain a balance between individual growth and growth as a couple. *Companionship* should be the adhesive that stabilizes your relationship, not a suffocating togetherness.

6. Continue to foster a healthy sexual relationship. Sex can be a wonderful expression of love and concern for each other, while continuing to be creative and exciting in its expression.

7. Make friends with people your own age *now*, so that these same friends can be a support to you, and you to them, when the kids are gone.

8. Evaluate your marriage relationship from time to time. Go to retreats, read books together, see a counselor together when a problem cannot be resolved, and be willing to make changes where necessary.

9. Evaluate your job in the same way. Take an assessment of where you are and where you are going. Nothing can cause a midlife crisis quicker than being dissatisfied with your job.

10. Don't be afraid to alter your lifestyle or to try something new. Often a change can be a wonderfully rewarding thing if both of you agree about it and are excited about the prospects.

Look on the bright side of the empty nest. As H. Norman Wright points out, "There can be fewer financial pressures, more freedom for recreation and travel, more time to build and enhance your marriage, freedom to make some major changes without affecting the children, and greater maturity to evaluate your life and its direction."

All who have children eventually face the empty nest, some with struggles and feelings of meaninglessness, others with anticipation of a new and challenging chapter in life. The choice is up to you.

RESOURCES

Seasons of a Marriage. H. Norman Wright. Regal Books, 1982.

QUESTION 40

What is the best way to care for my aging parents?

Often there are guilt feelings associated with how to deal with aging parents. Mixed emotions about what is best for the parent, what is affordable, and what is realistic for you and your family can complicate your decision.

Let us consider some of the alternatives, along with important factors in making your decision.

1. *Independent living.* The ideal living experience for aging parents is where they can manage their own lives without intervention or other people's care. If your aging parent(s) live in an apartment or a home, are able to prepare most of their own meals, have interests to pursue, and have loved ones nearby, they should be left in that environment for as long as possible.

All of us like to be independent to pursue our own interests. This is certainly true for the elderly as well.

2. *Living with you.* This is where the guilt feelings come in. If your parents cannot take care of themselves, and you are considering taking them into your home, there are several things you need to consider.

John Gillies in his book *A Guide to Caring and Coping With Aging Parents* states, "Once upon a time, families did not move much. Wage-earners did not change jobs every two, three, or four years. Once upon a time, American families were mostly rural or lived in small towns. Their houses were big, could easily be enlarged, and the families were large. Once upon a time mothers stayed home. It was expected that Father and Mother, and Grandfather and Grandmother would end their years in their own homes. . . .

"Once upon a time, before the era of dozens of technological inventions to make home care and cooking easier, faster, and more efficient, there were enough essential chores for every member of the family."

Today's environment presents a new set of problems for caring for the elderly in your home.

First, how does your elderly parent feel about it? Do the children get on his or her nerves? Do you have a large enough house to give them their own space? Do both of you work? Is your aging parent left alone much of the time? How much medical/physical care does your aging parent need? How does your spouse feel about your parent living with you? How will this affect the harmony and chemistry of your family life? If your aging parent lives in another town, how disruptive will a major move be to where you live? What can you afford in parental care?

If you can solve these questions with a minimum of difficulty, then a logical solution for you could very well be to keep your aging parent in your home. Many families can still cope with this solution happily and successfully. However, if this is not an acceptable solution for you, don't fall into the trap of feeling guilty.

Remember that the guilt you may feel in placing your parent in outside care is not necessarily being felt by your aging parent. Companions, activities, and good health care in a professional facility may actually produce more happiness for your aging parent than living in a stressful situation in your home.

If the introduction of an aging parent into your home will create friction and disharmony in your family (for whatever reason), you must give consideration to your own family's needs and your own mental health.

3. *Retirement centers.* These are becoming more popular and available. These continue to provide independence for elderly people by giving them their own rooms but

supplementing their living experience by providing meals, activities, regular observation of their needs and health, and friends who live in the same facility.

While these facilities are often built next to convalescent centers or other medical facilities, they are not nursing homes. Some of them provide a "life care" guarantee which includes future nursing care if and when needed.

4. *Nursing homes.* These provide the constant care needed for elderly who no longer have the ability to care for themselves. There is a place for them in our society. However, great care needs to be taken in selecting a nursing home.

Some of these are unethical, fraudulent, and almost inhumane in the way they treat their elderly patients.

Careful investigation should include: interview of the staff; inspection of the facilities; observation of the overall health and happiness of current residents; inspection of the room, recreational facilities, activities offered, meals (ask to eat one yourself), licensing, and cost.

5. *Other options.* There are some other options, depending on your circumstances and financial capabilities. These include live-in nursing, day care centers, and group care opportunities.

Whatever you decide, you should continue to support your parent with love and concern. Don't be motivated by guilt but by genuine concern for the most comfort, happiness, and emotional adjustment for your family, your parent, and yourself.

When asking my own mother-in-law about the choices in caring for the elderly she said, "If I get too feeble to care for myself, I prefer going to a nursing home but I want my kids to come and see me. I don't want to be forgotten."

RESOURCES

A Guide to Caring and Coping With Aging Parents. John Gillies. Thomas Nelson Publishers, 1981.

Growing Old Is a Family Affair. Dorothy Bertulet Fritz. John Knox Press, 1976.
I Chose to Live in a Nursing Home. Opal Hutchins Sollenberger. David C. Cook, 1980.

QUESTION 41

I have children still at home but I'm considering going back to work. Should I or shouldn't I?

This is a very controversial subject today. Working mothers are a fact. Some work because of divorces, widowhood, or financial burdens too big for one paycheck. Others simply enjoy a career and feel better being a working woman.

The right answer for you has a lot to do with your circumstances. Let's first discuss the ideal situation. We believe that those women who have a choice should seriously consider staying home with their children during their adolescent years. These are critical years for your child's overall development, and a loving home environment with a mother who can take time to play, pray, love, and experience her kids can make a significant difference in the child's development.

It may sound corny and old-fashioned in today's society, but we believe that women who make their family their first priority are the backbone of the family structure.

One retired first-grade teacher said, "After 41 years in the classroom, the one thing that stands out is that the most well-adjusted children usually came from homes where the mothers made a career of their family."[1]

There is a popular notion in some circles today that "homemakers" are not whole people, somehow missing out on the real stuff of life. Professor Kathryn E. Walker of Cornell University conducted a survey which reveals that if the services which women perform at home had to be purchased from outsiders the cost would be $28,000 a year at 1980 wages. Today it would be even more. A homemaker's work involves laundering, cooking, cleaning, and mending; caring for, dressing, feeding, guiding, and tutoring young children; sending out cards and letters, and keeping several people's appointment calendars; involvement in PTA, community services, taxi services, and a host of other volunteer jobs. Add to this the role of nutritionist, psychologist, spiritual counselor, director of finances, and you've got a lot of talent and a very valuable executive in that apron!

If you opted to stay home, don't feel left out. You are performing a wonderful service that will someday pay huge dividends. Consider yourself privileged to be part of a dying breed in America. Your efforts will last for generations.

On the other hand, if you must work, all hope is not lost. God understands your circumstances and can help you make up the difference. Here are some tips that will help you compensate for having a full-time job outside the home. These are quoted from an article by Gloria Foster (a working mother) titled "Work Full-time and Enjoy Your Kids Too" (*Virtue* magazine, September/October 1980):

1. *Make time to be alone with each child.* "Lo, children are a heritage of the Lord" (Psalm 127:3).

Sharon and I take turns reading chapters of her books. She also enjoys helping with the menu planning and cooking. I watch her limber body glide through the movements of an interpretive dance. We clean her fishbowl and rabbit cage together. She sings as I play the piano.

Gregg helps me with the grocery shopping on weekends. We often stop for coffee and Coke and just talk. I hear what's on his mind and how school is going.

Sometimes I flop on his bed and listen to his latest album. It isn't always my favorite kind of music. But it's important to me to know what is important to him. At the end of the day I rub his back.

Shirley and I eat lunch out when our schedules permit. We have good visits without the interruptions of the busy household. At other times we shop for a new dress, or else fabric with which to sew a dress.

I pop into her bedroom. "Listen to this!" she exclaims, and reads a passage from her literature text. Suddenly my mind whisks me back to a college classroom of more than 20 years ago. I too studied Keats.

We read Scripture and talk about how we can share God's love with others. Recently I shared letters with Shirley that I wrote to her and tucked away while she was growing up. She gains insights into how I thought and felt as a younger woman. It brings us closer.

Shirley may leave the nest soon. This makes our time together even more precious.

Gary and I have a regular Saturday date driving to his piano lessons. He brings me his latest robot design. "This is how it will work," he says in a serious voice. I marvel at the intricacies of his plan. As an artistic person, he thinks a lot. But he is happy to share his thoughts when I express interest in them.

Most of the ideas shared above take little of my time. It is not the amount of time that is important, but how meaningful it is for us. Those moments alone help me appreciate the God-given uniqueness of each of my children, my "heritage from the Lord."

2. *Keep the channels of communication open.* "Incline thine ear unto wisdom, and apply thine heart to understanding" (Proverbs 2:2).

Communication includes a feeling of acceptance, of being understood. It is easy to block those channels if I am not careful.

When Shirley wants to talk or Gary has something to show me, I try to be available. These moments can be as elusive as butterflies and easily lost. Sometimes it is an interruption of my own project. I may even feel a twinge of impatience. But listening to the small things brings them back when more important concerns fill their minds and hearts.

I encourage them to be honest and to feel free to disagree

with me. If I am willing to admit error or reconsider a decision, I find that they are too.

During the children's earlier years I talked much—to train, discipline, and teach. Now I listen much—to share, learn, and gain insights into their lives. I ask the Lord often to help me "incline mine ear and apply mine heart."

3. *Turn a negative situation into a positive one.* "A word fitly spoken is like apples of gold in pictures of silver" (Proverbs 25:11).

Fatigue and frustration can set in at the end of the work or school day. Disappointments cause one family member to strike out against another. Children do not always meet their responsibilities. When this happens, I try not to overreact. This drains me of the energy I need to cope with the situation.

I might walk in from a hectic day to find teenage bodies sprawled in front of the television. Homework texts lie unopened on the table. Dishes balance precariously on the sink. The trash overflows.

The kids' eyes meet mine. "I was going to clean the kitchen after this program," one hastily volunteers. "The trash cans are already full," adds another.

"What's for dinner?" asks Sharon, her eyes still glued to the screen.

I take a deep breath and think of the pluses. They are responsible enough to care for themselves. They get along well together in my absence. They are willing to help when I remind them that I am working for them and need their help in return.

I can't really expect them to carry on the household like I would. Things will be broken. Instructions will be misunderstood or ignored. But if I remember the pluses, my "words fitly spoken" can bring positive results.

4. *Make time for yourself.* "Create in me a clean heart, O God, and renew a right spirit within me" (Psalm 51:10).

I cannot continually give to my family if my own reservoir is not frequently replenished. Here are some ways through which I do this.

A. I have a physical space to call my own. It is simply a desk and bookcase in my bedroom, but I ask that it be respected by my family.

B. A scented bath recharges me. I often read while I soak.

C. I enjoy walking. It is rare when I don't see something in God's creation to delight me.

D. I rise a bit earlier or stay up a little later than the family. That first cup of coffee in the early dawn and those quiet moments in Bible study at the end of the day are equally delicious!

E. It is a treat to stop during errands and buy myself lunch. And there's no mess to clean up!

F. A library has built-in quiet. It is a great place to catch up on reading and letter-writing.

G. My newest interest is pressing flowers. The infinite patterns in God's floral creations are amazing!

H. I try to eat dinner out monthly with a sister or friend. The companionship of women I am close to is refreshing.

I. Now and then I enroll in a local night class. A recent law course netted helpful legal information as well as several new acquaintances. (I also dropped a class when I found that it fragmented my life rather than enriched it.)

I do not view taking time for myself as selfishness or withdrawal. It is necessary reinforcement of my God-given individuality. I need time alone to "renew the right spirit within me."

Good communication, turning the negative into positive, and making time for each child alone and for myself strengthens our family relationships. Knowing that the Lord is my ever-faithful Partner as I balance family and working, I can "rejoice and be glad."

If you can stay home during your child's adolescence, we encourage you to do so. If you cannot, ask for God's help to give the extra effort to make your home a haven.

RESOURCES

When Mom Goes to Work. Mary Beth Master. Moody Press, 1980.
When You Both Go to Work. Louis and Kay Moore. Word Books, 1982.

NOTES

1. Judy Hammersmark, "Happy at Home," in the July/August 1980 issue of *Virtue* magazine.

Part X

Friendship & In-Laws

QUESTION 42

> **Ugly words and circumstances have broken a good friendship. How can we put the pieces back together?**

Ruth Senter in *The Seasons of Friendship* gives a graphic picture of friends who have hurt us deeply.

> . . . as the earth tracks through space and the years replace one another, you remember disappointment. Your adult mind reminds you what happens when you trust someone. They build you up to let you down, take your hopes and give them back to you in an empty paper bag. Friends seem to be what they are not and are not what they seem to be. You give yourself to them with no second thoughts. Pure trust. No cross-examination. No scrutiny. You take them for what they seem. You believe in their authenticity. But only until reality catches up with you and shows you a different picture. Then a friend lets you down. You blame yourself for your naivete, your friend for inconsistency. You reject act and actor, deed and doer. And you remember that you were let down once before.
>
> And in your current disappointment you determine it will never happen again. Next time no one is going to mislead you. You will not give them the chance. You become a skeptic; you rechart your course to compensate for your diminished faith in people. Once you gave without reservation. Now you reserve the right to add up the risk, cross-examine the motives, check out the loopholes, weigh the returns. Once you expected the best; now you imagine the worst. Once you gave the benefit of the doubt; now you simply doubt.[1]

Friendship and love always involve risk. We have to put our hearts and emotions on the line. We become vulnerable. That's the nature of a close friendship. Close friendships are actually love relationships. And here's what the apostle Paul says about a true love relationship: "Love is very patient and kind, never jealous or envious, never boastful or proud, never haughty or selfish or rude. Love does not demand its own way. It is not irritable or touchy. It does not hold grudges and will hardly even notice when others do it wrong. It is never glad about injustice, but rejoices whenever truth wins out. If you love someone you will be loyal to him no matter what the cost. You will always believe in him, always expect the best of him, and always stand your ground in defending him" (1 Corinthians 13:4-7 TLB).

The first thing we must assess in any strained or broken relationship is what that friendship is worth. We must try to filter through our feelings of hurt and betrayal to realize that friendships are hard to come by. Think of the hours and days of intimate building that have taken place between you and your friend. Think of the emotions of alienation that she is feeling as well. Remember that Jesus was betrayed, and yet He did not forsake, castigate, or write off those who betrayed Him. Just what is that friendship worth to you? Is it worth your pride? Is it worth losing the argument, giving up the object, letting your friend save face by winning, forgetting the hurtful words and the betrayal? It probably is, and if you can be the one to make the first move, it will not only restore a broken friendship but make you a better person.

Basically there is one tough and difficult step in restoring a broken relationship: forgiveness. You must initiate (regardless of who is at fault) the extension of forgiveness. Go the second, the third mile. See your friend for the value you know is in your relationship. Yes, that means a willingness to swallow pride and hurt, to put your trust and emotions back out in the open, where they run the risk of being hurt again. Remember, friendship involves vulnerability and risk. You will have to take the risky steps to reestablish the relationship.

It means olive branches, courting, humor, repentance, and genuine acts of love.

An unknown author wrote: "To love at all is to be vulnerable. Love anything and your heart will certainly be wronged and possibly be broken. If you want to make sure of keeping it intact, you must give your heart to no one. Wrap it carefully with baubles and little luxuries, avoid all entanglements, lock it safe in a casket of your own selfishness. There it will not be broken. It will become unbreakable, impenetrable, irredeemable."

If you have crossed this first step of being willing to risk again, being willing to be vulnerable again, here are some practical steps to take in restoring the relationship.

1. *Ask God to help you forget the past.* It is no doubt true that we can never really *forget* the past. But what can happen is to frame it in a perspective of growth and love. This has a way of taking the hurt, making it less painful, and giving you a better perspective on it. God has a way of keeping you from spending all your days and nights dwelling on the details and the pain. Give it up to God and He will begin the process of putting the hurt to rest. New joys in the friendship will quickly anesthetize the pain you are now feeling.

2. *Keep the friendship in perspective.* True friendships are never built when one person brings a greater sense of dependency to the relationship than the other. Andre Bustanoby, marriage and family therapist, writes that intimate friendships "involve a reciprocal commitment to meet each other's emotional needs. For example, to sit quietly, sharing joys and sorrows, tracing with the other person's emotional state of mind. It also includes the ongoing affirmation of that person. . . . The key word is *reciprocal*, a two-way emotional commitment." He goes on to say that when one party in a friendship is making need-love demands that the other party in the friendship does not want to fulfill, you have a one-sided relationship where one party to the

friendship has needs and is making demands, while the other party does not have the same needs and considers the demands as responsibility.

Dr. James Dobson in his book *Love Must Be Tough* states that when this happens in a marriage, one partner begins to feel trapped in the relationship. One-sided friendships make one feel equally as trapped.

Recognize that the friendship must be a) reciprocal and b) kept in perspective. Keeping it in perspective means that we must recognize the other things in the person's life besides this particular friendship, such as other friends, possibly a marriage, work associates, hobbies, relatives, and other involvements that make up life.

You and your friend need to give each other room to breathe and freedom to pursue other people and interests outside your friendship.

3. *Learn to be a giver and a listener.* This parallels very closely the item we just discussed about reciprocal friendship, but it is more the technique of fostering a friendship. Scripture says, "Give and it shall be given unto you; pressed down, shaken together, and running over shall men give unto your bosom" (Luke 6:38). There is a definite principle of giving that works wonders in any relationship. Learn the principle that it is indeed "more blessed to give than to receive." Always be looking for ways you can give to the friendship, in the form of time, patience, love, and a listening ear.

Being a good listener is a wonderful gift, and yet few of us make much effort to cultivate it. Most of us are talkers, communicators. We want our own ideas and feelings to be heard, but few of us are willing to listen.

When I did my graduate work in counseling psychology part of our major course work was to enter into counseling situations with permission to record the sessions. The recordings were later played back by a group of my professors and critiqued as to my counseling technique. Up until that time I thought I was a good listener. However, week after week my professors would critique my tapes with the same concern: "You are not *listening* to what this person is really saying"; "you are not hearing what he is telling you"; "you are giving advice she is not asking for"; "you are dominating the conversation." Yes, I finally satisfied my professors and became a better listener, but not without some agonizing personal evaluation on how little I really listened to other people.

Listening sounds simple, but it is a rare and wonderful gift that takes practice. In fact, I think the gift of listening is more difficult to cultivate than eloquent speech, and a whole lot more needed in our society. Listening involves more than hearing words. It involves eye contact, concern, discernment, paying attention to emotions, caring, feeling what the other person is feeling, watching for underlying motives and for facial expressions (that show empathy, acceptance, and attentiveness), and asking the right questions at the appropriate time to encourage the person to go deeper into their feelings and concerns.

You may not possess all these skills now, but if you *practice* listening you can become greatly skilled at the art. The gift of being a listener does not require a degree—only the willingness to be there, to keep quiet, and to feel genuine concern.

Here are some things to watch very carefully and guard against. These are common circumstances that can strain any friendship.

1. When one person demands more from the friendship than the other person is willing to deliver.

2. When a person offers advice that is unasked-for and is presumed to be attempting to dominate the friendship.

3. When friends go into business together or one loans money to the other.

4. When one betrays the confidence of a friend to a third person (even when it is presumed to be in the friend's best interest) and the friend discovers the betrayal.

5. When one participates in practical jokes or humor of which your friend is the object.

While these do not automatically result in the loss of a friendship, they are quite common factors in the dissolution of close friendships. They are also some of the same pitfalls that can potentially destroy a marriage.

RESOURCES

The Seasons of Friendship. Ruth Senter. Zondervan, 1982.
It Feels Good to Forgive. Helen Hosier. Harvest House Publishers, 1980.

NOTES

1. Taken from *The Seasons of Friendship* by Ruth Senter. Copyright © 1982 Zondervan Corp. Used by permission.

QUESTION 43

I don't have any close friends and I feel lonely. How can I develop friendships?

In this answer we are discussing two interrelated issues: loneliness and friendship. Let's first discuss loneliness, along with problems of intimacy, and then ways to develop intimate friendships.

First, let's recognize the difference between being alone and feeling lonely. Everyone needs "space" from time to time. Being alone can be a healthy and welcome experience. That is not the same as feeling lonely. One can feel deep loneliness while with a crowd of people.

Loneliness is an emotion that affects millions of Americans. Some try to fill the vacuum with partying, going to bars, having illicit sex, or going on all forms of "mind trips" (pop psychology, Eastern religions, etc.).

One survey indicated that nearly 30 percent of America's adult population had feelings of loneliness within a two-week period. Widowed and divorced persons felt most lonely, followed by single adults. A surprisingly large percentage of married people were included, with married women expressing loneliness predominately over married men.

Each of us has at least two basic needs: the need to be loved and the need to belong. If either (or both) of these needs is not being met, loneliness will result. The authors of *Why Be Lonely?* list five general causes of loneliness, based on the Bible and psychiatric experience. They are: 1) isolation from God; 2) our changing society; 3) rejecting others;

4) rejection by others; and 5) neglect in childhood. Let's look at each of these.

1. *Isolation from God.* Scripture teaches that there is a void or vacuum in each of us that can only be filled by a personal relationship with Jesus Christ. We may attempt to fill this void with many other things, but the end result is more loneliness and disillusionment until we come face-to-face with the reality of Jesus Christ.

From time to time even Christians will feel this loneliness when fellowship with God is neglected or broken. Eve experienced that loneliness the moment she ate of the forbidden fruit. David the psalmist experienced loneliness after his willful sin with Bathsheba. Feelings of loneliness for Christians are only feelings or perceptions, because God has said, "I will *never* leave you or forsake you" (Hebrews 13:5).

2. *Our changing society.* Our American lifestyle promotes loneliness: frequent uprooting, with moves to different parts of the country; crowded neighborhoods, with high-fenced yards, double-bolted doors, and little contact with those who sleep and eat just 25 feet away; television-watching, which robs us of meaningful conversation and teaches us to trust other people even less; and individualistic, independent role models—all of these contribute to loneliness.

3. *Rejecting others.* Many of us are hesitant to be open and vulnerable with other people for fear of being rejected. In an effort to avoid the pain of rejection, we reject others first.

4. *Rejection by others.* We've all been "burned" by what we thought was a friend. The pain of being rejected by other people leads us to protect our vulnerability and be wary of others' overtures to friendship.

5. *Neglect in childhood.* Divorce, fathers too busy with careers, ugly words spoken about us as a child by teachers or peers, parents' mispunishment in attacking our character—all lend to withdrawal and deep feelings of loneliness.

When we allow these things to creep into our lives, the result is a source of loneliness and loss of intimacy. Any close personal friendship requires risking vulnerability and intimacy (including development of closeness in marriage).

Often we avoid intimacy because we don't like ourselves very much. We subconsciously reason that if we don't like ourselves, other people won't either. We think, "If people only knew what I was really like, they would reject me" or we have feelings of not being good enough to meet another intimate friendship.

So we avoid intimacy by being occupied with work, sports, or hobbies, or by using sarcasm when someone gets too close, or by substituting sex or other forms of behavior for true intimacy.

All of these are attempts to ease the pain of loneliness, but they are substitutes that have little or no lasting effects.

In addition, there are other emotions that are used to demonstrate our loneliness. Two of these are anger and depression. Anger is a defense mechanism that is often triggered by deep feelings of loneliness. It is a way of expressing bitterness, rebellion, or resentment for the deep feelings of loneliness, while simultaneously holding other people away from us.

Depression is usually prompted by a feeling of separation and isolation from other people. Depression comes when our hope for meaningful and intimate relationships is gone.

All of these causes of loneliness must be dealt with if we are going to experience intimate friendships. We must be willing to risk love and vulnerability in order to gain a close friendship. In John 15:9-15 we read a profound and touching narrative from Jesus:

> As the Father loved Me, I also have loved you; abide in My love. If you keep My commandments, you will abide in My love, just as I have kept My Father's commandments and abide in His love.
> These things I have spoken to you that My joy may remain in you, and that your joy may be full. This is My commandment, that you love one another as I have loved you.

Greater love has no one that this, than to lay down one's life for his friends. You are My friends if you do whatever I command you.

No longer do I call you servants, for a servant does not know what his master is doing; but I have called you friends, for all things that I heard from My Father I have made known to you (NKJV).

Jesus was our example in His willingness to risk everything, including life itself for His friends. This is "risk" and "vulnerability" at its best! In another place Jesus told us to be willing to forgive others seventy times seven in one day (Matthew 18:21,22). Only in our willingness to put ourselves on the line and to risk being rejected can we ever experience the true joys of intimate friendship.

Here are some ways to overcome loneliness and develop meaningful friendships.

1. *Take the initiative.* Don't sit around and wait for someone to knock on your door and ask if she can become your friend. *You* invite someone for dinner or to an activity! Meet someone for coffee. Join a ministry or activity that will keep you in contact with other people. While activity alone will not produce friends, it will put you in contact with people and open doors for friendships.

2. *Risk loving others.* Tim Timmons states in his book *Loneliness Is Not a Disease*: "True love carries a high level of identification with the loved ones . . . an ability to reveal intimate thoughts, feelings, and suggestions, as well as a general tendency toward self-disclosure. Love brings the plight of empathy, emotional understanding, and sympathetic orientation toward the loved ones. Love is a decision to relate, comfort, and encounter the loved ones honestly, frankly, and without inhibition."

3. *Strengthen your love relationship to God.* God is love. Scripture tells us that this perfect love casts out fear, and Jesus in John 15 says that we are no longer servants but friends. God is the Author of love and friendship; in an intimate relationship with Him, we can conquer

loneliness and learn the art of friendship.

When there is more of the character of Christ in us (love, joy, peace, longsuffering, patience, goodness), other people will be attracted to us, and intimate friendships will be easier to develop and maintain.

4. *Accept other people's imperfections.* Nobody is perfect. If you expect others to never make a mistake, never be touchy, never say the wrong thing, or never express anger, you will be disappointed. A critical or evaluating nature that keeps another person on trial will never produce a relaxed, caring environment in which an intimate friendship can flourish. In many ways, intimate friendship both inside and outside marriage must take someone "for better, for *worse*, for richer, for *poorer*, in *sickness* and in health." It's the unconditional "you-don't-have-to-be-anything-other-than-you" kind of acceptance that builds intimate friendships.

5. *Learn to be a giver and forgiver.* Paul tells us in 1 Corinthians 13 that love "hardly even notices when others do it wrong" (TLB). Be quick to forgive and forget. Constantly be on the lookout for ways to give to the other person. In this way she will not feel smothered by your demands to fulfill your personal needs. Give your friend the freedom to be herself, to be with other people apart from you, to have a life of her own.

6. *Learn the art of touching.* Healthy forms of touching and hugging can be like a tonic to a friend. All of us need to be touched. Someone has said that we need at least eight hugs a day to be healthy! Often a tender touch can bring you closer to someone than a thousand words. Touching does not need to have erotic connotations. It can simply be a way of expressing care, concern, comfort, and warmth. It is a powerful way to say "You're special!"

7. *Learn to be honest.* Never play word games or "emotional leapfrog" with a friend. Be frank and honest. Care enough to confront your friend with your concerns and hurts in a nonaccusatory way. Openness and honesty on the part

of two people, when surrounded by love, acceptance, and forgiveness, will only strengthen the relationship. (Read Question #42 for more insights into developing healthy friendships.)

RESOURCES

Psalm 25:16-18; Isaiah 41:10; 43:2; Matthew 28:20.
Why Be Lonely? Leslie Canter, Paul D. Meier, and Frank B. Minirth. Baker Book House, 1982.
Loneliness Is Not a Disease. Tim Timmons. Harvest House Publishers, 1981.
For All Your Seasons. Carnegie Samuel Calian. John Knox Press, 1979.
The Seasons of Friendship. Ruth Senter. Zondervan, 1982.

QUESTION 44

> ## I have a hard time liking my mother-in-law. How can things improve?

Feelings of this nature are often experienced by young brides. After all, a mother-in-law can be threatening. Who else knows your sweetheart as she does? Who loved him first? Who can create those famous German pancakes while you're still struggling with scrambled eggs? The mother-in-law can be built up in your mind to be quite a formidable foe. In one sense she's the "other woman." But as your marriage matures, *those feelings need to mature.*

To put your mind at ease: She doesn't want him back! (If she does, she's most unusual!) Most mothers are aware that someday "sonny boy" will come home with a glazed look in his eye and Mom will know that he has met *the one.* The wise mother will have been praying for that special young woman that her son will someday marry. She will know when to cut the cord and let her son go. But other mothers find it more difficult. I have observed that some women go through their "life stages" more gracefully than others. I remember the first day of school one year when I found a friend of mine sobbing outside the school, "My life is over!" She had just put her son in kindergarten. I confess I was feeling quite carefree that day!

Perhaps your mother-in-law is insecure in herself or in her own marriage. Her whole identity may be wrapped up in her children. This kind of mother-in-law can be interpreted as being "interfering" or "meddling." She needs love, understanding, and tactful honesty from you. For her own benefit as well as yours, she must learn that she cannot hold onto patterns of the past.

Dr. Norm Wright says, "Many young people enter into marriage eager to break away from a physical dependence upon their parents, but are unable to break their emotional dependence. The resulting conflict is intensified by society's expectations that married people be independent of their parents. When this conflict is unresolved, a young married person may feel a growing competition between his spouse, his spouse's parents, and his own parents."[1]

After you are married, you should find that your relationship with your parents becomes a friendship—a deep, caring, respectful friendship. Emotional dependence between adults should be reserved for marriage. Genesis 2:24 says, "A man shall leave his father and his mother and shall cleave unto his wife, and they shall be one flesh."

The mother is a key factor in allowing her children to "leave and cleave." If a woman has a hard time doing this it is because her emotional needs are fulfilled by her children's dependence on her.

In rearing our own children, we have tried to prepare them for independence. This is bittersweet . . . something you don't understand as a young bride. A mother can see her child's independence as a "death knell": It's all over. She has invested her heart and life in her child, and now he's gone. Our greatest aim in life as parents should be to transfer the youthful hands that now hold ours into God's.

Here are some questions to ask yourself.

1. *How is my own marriage?* How is the communication developing between me and my husband? Do I let him know my needs and feelings? How well do I understand him? Do I have the communication skills to honestly let him know my frustration and desires regarding my in-laws? Do we create our own premium "space" together—not constantly being with relatives and friends?

2. *Do I respect my husband's family?* Sometimes the rejection of your in-laws may be a subtle rejection of your spouse.

Part of acceptance is "warts and all"—loving *in spite of*, not necessarily *because of*. I have heard many young women criticize their mothers-in-law. I think sometimes it's sheer habit, the thing to do. But it's a damaging habit. The Scriptures that deal with gossip, backbiting, and unkindness apply to our family relationships as well. The more we complain, the bigger the problem becomes in our own minds.

3. *Am I making her problem my problem?* Sometimes when people are difficult, and you do as much as you can to help the relationship, nothing seems to work! At some point you must do what you know you must, and not constantly try to please your mother-in-law. Your lives should not be centered around your in-laws' lives. Make plans with couples your own age. Plan activities together as a couple.

4. *What am I expecting from my mother-in-law?* Are you subconsciously comparing your mother-in-law to your own mother? She doesn't keep house like your mother, she doesn't cook like your mother, she celebrates holidays differently, and yet you call her "Mother." Seems strange, doesn't it? Remember that your husband's mother is not your own mother. Respect and love her for who she is: your sweetheart's mother. There is a certain amount of commitment that you make to your husband's family when you make a commitment to him—a commitment of love and respect—but this doesn't mean that you should be *engulfed* by your husband's family, nor he by yours. Both of you need to carve out your own family, using material from both of your families to create a unique family.

5. *What kind of mother-in-law do I want to be someday?* What would you like from your future daughter-in-law (or son-in-law)? Put yourself in your mother-in-law's place. Remembrance of special days, phone calls, letters, snapshots of the children—all these thoughtful gestures do much to build the relationship. Your mother-in-law has invested much of her life in your husband, and she cares deeply about your family. It is her love and work that has made your husband the man he is—the man you felt was the best in the

whole world. Invite her to special functions with you—shopping trips, luncheons, ladies' meetings. Pray for her. Ask God to give you His insight toward her.

Holiday celebrations can be trying when there is tension in relationships. Be fair about spending what-holiday-with-whom-when! You may end up offending somebody in spite of your best efforts, but keep your sense of humor. Love always wins out in the end. Before too many years you'll be in the driver's seat, and it will be your home where the celebrations are held. Build on that relationship *now*. Your mother-in-law has a lot to offer you. Don't waste these years by not seeing her for what she can be—a treasured friend.

RESOURCES

How to Be a Better Than Average In-Law. H. Norman Wright. Victor Books, 1981.

Mother-in-Laws Can Be Fun. Lou Beardsley. Harvest House Publishers, 1981.

NOTES

1. *How to Be a Better Than Average In-Law.* H. Norman Wright. Victor Books, 1981.